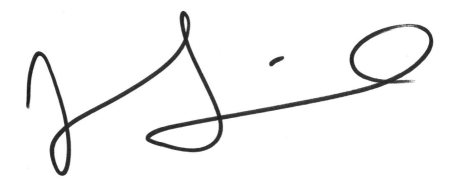

DREAMCATCHER

JUDE SCHIMMEL
with Richard Laemmle

Edited by: Kristen M. Lutes
Graphic Design: F. Scott Scinta
Cover Photo: Michelle Elliot

Printed in the United States of America.

First Edition, 2015

ISBN 978-0-9962671-0-6 (softcover)
ISBN 978-0-9962671-1-3 (hardcover)

22i Publishing
3011 McMahan Boulevard
Louisville, KY 40220
www.22ipublishing.com

DEDICATION

To my parents, Rick and Ceci, to my seven siblings Shae, Shoni, Job, Milan, Mick, Saint and Sun, and to my three grandmothers Sis, Delores, and Jane. You all have helped me get to where I am today and I am eternally grateful to have you all as family. To Cicily and Sam, my closest friends, thank you for always being there.

To Indian country and Native Americans across the country who have inspired me to become the person and role model I am striving to be.

To everyone else who has made a difference in my life, thank you for the lessons and experiences you've given me that have helped shape me into the person I am today. To anyone who has ever had the hope of achieving a dream, to anyone who has ever had the hope of living a positive, healthy, happy, successful life, and to those who believe in change.

SPECIAL THANKS

Special thanks to the following people for helping make my vision become a reality.
Thank you all for sharing your time, talents, input, and encouragement. JS

Angie Laemmle

Jessica Laemmle

Jenna Laemmle

Julia Laemmle

Jenn Esteban

Arica Carter

Scott Scinta

Jonathan Hock

Shoni Schimmel

Michelle Elliot

Lee Michaelson

Robert Sampson

Kris Lutes

Frank Battafarano

Joel Day

University of Louisville Athletics

TABLE OF CONTENTS

PART I: MY STORY

PART II: MY LESSONS

PART III: MY PEOPLE

CONCLUSION

Photo Courtesy Lee Michaelson

I'm very, very, very proud of you guys. Sometimes when you win, you really lose. And sometimes when you lose, you really win. Look where you've come from. Look what you've done. Each and every one of us, we are going to succeed, and good things are going to come your way. But you have to make them happen. You have to believe. Go out and strive in life. Go out and do well. Go out and lead. You do it. And come back and change the world. Make the world fair. Make the world good. Make the world happy. - Mom

PART 1: MY STORY

INTRODUCTION

The clock showed 2.6 seconds left to play.

On March 31, 2013, we were playing the Baylor Bears in the NCAA® tournament regional semi-finals in Oklahoma City in a nationally televised game on ESPN. Baylor entered the game as the top overall seed of the tournament, the defending national champions, and one of the best teams of all time. Baylor was on a 32-game winning streak, had won 74 of their past 75 games, and they were 27-point favorites over us that night.

My team, the Louisville Cardinals, had executed our coaching staff's game plan to perfection throughout the whole game. I had contributed two three-pointers, five rebounds, and three assists in twenty-eight minutes of play. My sister Shoni hit five threes and scored twenty-two points before fouling out with four minutes left to go in the second half. By containing Baylor's star Brittney Griner and hitting an NCAA record-tying sixteen three-pointers, my team had built a large lead during the game, lost the lead after a furious Baylor comeback, and then regained it at 82-81 with 2.6 seconds left to play. Baylor had the ball and would have one final shot to beat us.

As I stood on the court ready to defend the final seconds, I couldn't help but think of what this win would mean to so many people if we could hold on. Shoni was on the bench – an unfamiliar place for her with the game on the line. I was playing for her. I was playing for my teammates and coaches. I was playing for my family. I was playing for the city of Louisville. But mostly, I was playing for the entire Native American community.

Baylor inbounded the ball from their baseline to their point guard, she crossed half court, and drove towards us as she prepared to take the game's deciding shot as the clock was about to expire. My only concern at that point was to keep her from getting a good shot off. I lunged forward at her, threw my hands up, then backed off, making sure not to foul. I turned to watch the outcome of the ball in flight. It seemed like it was in slow motion.

The ball hit high off the backboard, then fell to the floor.

Game Over.

Many have called it the greatest upset in the history of women's college basketball. To me, it was something much larger than that.

I immediately ran towards Shoni as the celebration began. Fans, coaches and players were all celebrating wildly as they knew the impact that this basketball victory would have on our season and for the entire Louisville program. I jumped into Shoni's arms and gave her the biggest emotion-filled hug I've ever given anyone in my life.

What the nation saw with that embrace was a celebration of a big basketball upset victory. What people didn't understand was that it was really a celebration of overcoming years of adversity, overcoming years of prejudice, and overcoming years of people telling us we couldn't succeed because we were Native Americans. The moment represented all of our years of hard work, all of the lessons of mental toughness our parents taught us, and all of the years of sacrifices that our parents made to allow us the opportunity to succeed. Through our basketball success, we had become role models to the entire Native American community. This moment was for all Native Americans everywhere to show them that you can go out and succeed in the world. It showed them that anything is possible if you make a goal and set your heart and mind to work hard for it. The victory also meant, as a result of a bet, that my parents would finally be getting married.

I am a Native American. This is my story of how I grew up on a reservation and had the values of the Native American culture instilled in me by previous generations. It's my story of how my dedicated parents sacrificed to allow my siblings and me every possible opportunity to succeed. It's my story of how hard work, focus, and dedication allowed me a chance to earn a basketball scholarship to the University of Louisville and the chance to experience the world outside of reservation life. It's my story about the lessons I've learned along the way and my advice to others on how to succeed. It's my hope that my story can inspire people by showing them anything is possible if you put your heart and mind to it.

I'm writing this book because I truly, truly want to see change. Reservation life is extremely sheltered and limiting for Native Americans, and in a sense it can be hard to escape. Native Americans have a hard time leaving their reservations and succeeding in the so called "real world." There is an untold number of Native Americans who are very gifted and talented, yet the overwhelming majority of them never make the most of their full potential. On my reservation, which is known as the Umatilla Indian Reservation, despite having a number of talented basketball players over the years, no one had ever received a college scholarship for basketball until my sister and I came along. Native Americans in general are stuck in a cycle of negativity across the nation. There are numerous reasons for this, including the brutality and uneasiness of the past, the inequality and oppression forced upon them for generations, and the simple lack of opportunities due to the culture of isolated reservation life. I want to share my story to show other Native Americans that you can overcome all of these things.

Native Americans are a beautiful people who have been oppressed and stuck in this cycle for far too long. Native Americans are strong and passionate and I want the rest of the world to understand that so they can truly get a sense of our essence. I want to see Native Americans across the country become successful. I want to see them live happy and healthy lives. I want them to change the negative cycle that has been holding them back for so many years. The prevailing mindset in Native American culture is that it is nearly impossible for them to break out of their comfort zones and succeed in various walks of life. Native Americans are conditioned to fail and are afraid to take chances in the outside world. I know this because I have experienced it and witnessed it for myself. It is easy for Native Americans to be content and comfortable with life on the reservation.

But I want them to read my story and see that it is possible for them to live the life of their dreams. I also think there are many lessons people from any background can learn from my experiences.

I also want to help the rest of the world understand Native Americans. I want to see Native Americans show the world who and what we really are. Like many other minorities, Native Americans have been unfairly stereotyped across the country. Through my travels and experiences I've met a lot of good, smart, non-Native people who were uneducated about the Native American culture and what we stand for. I've witnessed firsthand the negative stereotypes associated with Native Americans, and I hope to be able to enlighten others on the true values and beauty of Native culture. I want others to see and understand the potential in Native Americans, and for others to know that we are just as deserving of a chance to live good, positive, and meaningful lives. We deserve to have opportunities in society, school, sports, and all other areas of life.

I didn't write this book because I think I have the answers to every problem or because I think I'm an expert on every in and out of Native American life. Rather, I wrote this book based upon the experiences

I've been through, the discrimination I've personally witnessed, the judgmental people I've met, the injustices I've encountered, the unfairness I've observed, and the hurt of so many people. I'm also writing it based upon the goodness of others that I've seen, the pride people have demonstrated towards my accomplishments, the genuinely kind people I've met from other cultures, the overwhelming respect shown for me and my family, and the support I've received from tens of thousands of Native Americans.

Most important, I want to continue to be a source of hope and inspiration to others. I've met and spoken to thousands of Native Americans, and I've seen the hope in their eyes. I see how badly many wish they could have an opportunity to go after their dreams and accomplish their own goals as I've done. I truly want every single person to have that opportunity and to realize that they can be successful. I am writing this book because I am tired of hearing excuses for why individuals shouldn't or can't succeed. I want others to realize that life is full of ups and downs, and that it will never be perfect. I want them to understand that it's okay not to have everything in perfect order all the time. I want to show them that my family and I have had our own share of struggles and challenges just as every family has. We've all been at low points, and have experienced high points as well. I myself have been through good times, and I've also been through very bad ones. But I've learned to see the hard times I've faced as challenges that helped me grow and adjust to the changes of society and life. A lot of credit goes to my parents for giving me opportunities, but I, like all, eventually had to take the reins for myself — and here I am now.

I once was simply a normal Native American child who grew up on a reservation just like so many others who will read this. I wasn't the smartest, the biggest, the most athletic, or the most talented. Instead I learned and implemented lessons such as the value of a strong work ethic, focus, goal-setting, and trusting my gut feeling to help set myself up for success. I hope whoever reads this realizes that these are things anyone can incorporate into their own lives in order to start working towards accomplishing any goal.

My hope is that this book will positively change and impact lives. I want society's perspective to change. I want people to change. I want people to understand. I want people to live positive, healthy, successful, and happy lives. If you take a step back and strip away all of people's differences in any culture, that's all anyone is really seeking: positivity, health, success, and happiness. My hope is that Native Americans who read this will begin to realize all of these things are within their own power.

This book tells my story of how I was able to venture off my reservation, break through barriers, overcome adversity, take some risks and go out and succeed in the world. I want to tell of my experiences and accomplishments. I want to do this not to brag, but rather to show examples of things that can be accomplished and experienced by anyone who is determined to achieve their goals. I want to tell you about my time at the University of Louisville and how it shaped me as well. Finally, I want to give my perspective and insight on the lessons I was taught that allowed me to do these things, as well as the lessons I learned from my own experiences. I don't claim to be an expert on anything, but this is what worked for me and what I know is out there for anyone who puts their heart and mind to it.

I want others to view my life as an example of a Native American who grew up on a reservation but still had values and goals to make something more of herself…and if I can do it, why can't they?

I chose to open this book with this quote from my mother:

I'm very, very, very proud of you guys. Sometimes when you win, you really lose. And sometimes when you lose, you really win. Look where you've come from. Look what you've done. Each and every one of us, we are going to succeed, and good things are going to come your way. But you have to make them happen. You have to believe. Go out and strive in life. Go out and do well. Go out and lead. You do it. And come back and change the world. Make the world fair. Make the world good. Make the world happy. – Mom

She said this to us after a tough loss in the Oregon 6A State Tournament. This quote was also featured in our family documentary *Off the Rez*. It is extremely significant to me because it's been her point of emphasis since I was a little kid, and the message has inspired me to become the person I am today. It's not a coincidence that my book is based around this idea. My mother raised me to be a good person, and everything she has taught me over the years is a huge reason why I wanted to write this book in the first place. As she has inspired me, I hope to inspire others to implement the meaning of this quote as well as the contents of this book into their own lives.

PART 1: MY STORY

_____

THE RESERVATION

It was a really, really, really, small house. And I come from a very big family. At any time we would have up to eleven family members living in our house on Cottonwood Lane in Oregon. Growing up, I never thought twice about the size of our house, or the number of people I shared it with. It was all that we needed – and it was home. And we were happy. I also never worried about what kind of car my parents drove or how much stuff we owned. I had a roof over my head, I had food on the table, I had clothes on my back, I was able to go to school, and I had a family that loved and cared for me. To me that was more than enough. I never thought twice about fancy or expensive things because I loved our big family, and our small house. And I loved the strong family closeness that the combination of these two things produced. The memories I have from my years at this house are, and always will be, some of the most cherished memories of my life.

Our home was on the Umatilla Indian Reservation in eastern Oregon. The reservation is home to approximately one thousand Native American families, and we were pretty much sheltered from the outside world. My reservation, as many Native reservations are, is very rural — both physically and socially. There is just a much different way of life there than in traditional towns, cities, and communities. My reservation is extremely small. There's not much to see except homes, open land, a few restaurants, a gas station, a casino, and a movie theater. There's also a small fire department, a health clinic, a church, a gym, and a museum that tells the history of our people. A few of these places weren't built until recent years, so the reservation seemed even less developed until then. Just to give an idea of how underdeveloped reservations can be, there are still no grocery stores, no banks, no malls and no libraries. Generally speaking, life on the reservation has some similarities to modern places, but it has its own unique feel, which I think is sincerely hard to understand unless it's personally experienced.

Reservation life was extremely simple and comfortable to my family and me – and for that matter for most Native Americans in general. On my reservation everyone knew everyone else. There really wasn't such a thing as a stranger because we all either knew of each other or at least knew of each other's families. There was an overwhelming feeling of sincere, general, and mutual trust on my reservation as well. There was also a feeling that we were always safe. When I was growing up, my siblings and I would play basketball outside until very late into the night, yet my parents never worried about our safety because everyone looked out for one another.

Reservation life is also associated with Native American traditions. I find it funny and slightly ignorant that many people still imagine Native Americans living in tipis and wearing traditional regalia outside of cultural ceremonies or for everyday life. Although times have greatly evolved and that's not the case anymore, our cultural heritage is still significant and meaningful. As in many other Native American communities, cultural traditions are still extremely important on my reservation. Even though sports took up most of our family's time while we were growing up on the reservation, our Native heritage still held a very important place in our hearts. When I was younger my grandma and my great grandma used to dress us up in traditional attire, and we would participate in our reservation's local pow wow. For those who may not know, pow wows are gatherings of Native Americans in circles of friendship. They include singing and dancing, and they are times for renewing Native American traditions and preserving the rich history and culture of American Indians. As a young girl I enjoyed taking part in my cultural traditions. It was actually a lot of fun and I really do miss it. But now that I'm older I still attend them as frequently as possible because of the significance it holds in my heart.

We would also participate in our town's annual rodeo, called the Pendleton Roundup, which is a week-long festival dating back to 1910 that includes rodeo events, pow wows, beauty pageants, and parades. It also included a night show that depicted the settling of the American West, and the early relationship between the cowboys and Indians. During this time, we would set up our tipi alongside a few hundred other Native American families. The Roundup was a week-long celebration of going back in time, but of course it's an altered version of the reality our ancestors went through. My family would also participate in tradition-rich berry picking events and go to the sweat lodge, which is the place of spiritual refuge and mental and physical healing. These events plus many more were extremely significant to our Native American culture and way of life.

Generally speaking, I had lots to be thankful for in the way that I grew up and through the traditions my family took part in on the reservation. These years have helped create the foundation of my entire life. I appreciate where I grew up and where I come from because it has significantly helped shape me into the person that I am today. It's also made me learn to appreciate everything that I've experienced in my life. The experiences I had growing up on the reservation are held close to my heart; from having my grandmas and auntie living nearby, to playing outside everyday with my siblings and cousins, to enjoying ourselves with simple pleasures such as hide and seek, basketball, football, tag, riding bikes, and climbing trees, to celebrating our rich cultural traditions. Through my years living on the reservation I truly learned to enjoy and appreciate the simple things in life.

PART 1: MY STORY

FAMILY

In telling about my family, I have to start with my mother. She is my hero. She was an example of a Native American who was stuck in the cycle of isolated reservation life that I previously mentioned, having stayed and lived on a reservation most of her life despite having immense talent. She was a great athlete, yet experienced discrimination firsthand and wasn't informed about her opportunities to receive a scholarship even though she earned and deserved one. She vowed not to let her kids be victims to the same struggles, and she didn't. Our entire family, Shoni, and I have become role models to Native Americans across the country. As the high profile athletes, Shoni and I receive a lot of the credit for this. However, it is truly my mother who fought and earned everything for my family and me – and she deserves every single ounce of the credit.

My mom is truly the strongest person I know. She's been through so much hurt and heartache, and I have no idea how she is still standing so tall. I believe that is a representation of how strong her heart is. She is faithful and knows that if her heart is good and she continues to have good intentions then she is on the right path and God will always take care of her and provide for her.

My mom taught me a lot of what I know when it comes to dealing with obstacles in life. She used to sit my siblings and me down for hours and just talk to us and teach us so many different things through stories and examples. The fact that she has so many qualities that can't be taught is the reason why I think she's such a special individual. I've learned so many life lessons from her and I am eternally grateful for having been blessed with a mother like her.

My father came from a completely different background: he was white, he was offered and made aware of his options, and he was the star athlete of the town. He earned an athletic scholarship to play baseball at Stanford University, but after a year he made the decision to return home because my Mom became pregnant with my oldest brother. He chose to make raising a family and supporting my mother his priority above everything else. He is also one of the strongest people I know and made countless sacrifices over the years to support us in everything that we ever did. He loves and supports my mom to the best of his ability. To me they're like the perfect team. My mom is the backbone of our family, and my dad is hers. Now they might disagree with that, but that's how I see it, and I love them for that. I can't explain how much I admire them as parents and I can only hope that someday I have the strength and courage to steer and raise my children as they have raised me.

They have been through a lot together and have had to endure many hardships along the way, ranging from overt discrimination, to the lack of support from their own family and friends, to the fear of having to make sacrifices for their children to provide them with opportunities for a better life. They've demonstrated resiliency, determination, sacrifice, and many other noble qualities for our good and wellbeing. When my parents began dating, many people looked down on their relationship because my Dad was white and my mother was Native American. It was often frowned upon for whites to date Native Americans at that time, and unfortunately this discriminatory mindset still exists in some people today. When my mother became pregnant with my oldest brother, many people treated my parents with unnecessary disrespect and even my own grandfather – my dad's father – disowned him and we didn't know our grandpa for many years, although we did reconcile years later. This is just one of many examples of the type of hardships my parents endured for us.

My relationship with my parents is probably very similar to others. It's unique and special and of course complex at times, but I love them both and I am so grateful for everything they've done for me ever since I was born. There have been times when my parents and I have disagreed on certain things but I never allow that to affect our relationship. I love both of my parents beyond any measure and I can't even begin to explain how lucky I am to have been raised by two such intelligent and gifted individuals.

My parents have always been completely selfless and concerned about the wellbeing of their children. I really admire that about them because not many parents are willing to do the things they did for my siblings and me. They sacrificed their time, money, and energy for my brothers, sisters and me so that we could have the chance to live happy and successful lives. They stood up for us whenever necessary. They supported us when we needed it most. They really seemed to do literally everything to benefit us. I still don't understand how they did all the things they did and still do just for our benefits. I was able to achieve a lot at a young age directly because of their guidance and because of the lessons they taught me. I skipped the 8th grade, I left the reservation, I graduated high school, I graduated college in three years, and I played in NCAA tournaments, ranging from Sweet Sixteen finishes to the National championship game. I also received the Elite 89 award for having the highest grade-point-average of any player in the Final Four in 2013; I was selected as one of *Glamour* Magazine's Top 10 College Women of 2014; I attended the ESPY awards in Los Angeles; I've been to Mexico, Japan and Canada; I've traveled across the country for basketball and for speaking engagements, and now I am currently working on my master's degree -- all by the age of 21. That to me is crazy. It's still surreal how far I've come, but I know without everything my parents did for me and my family I wouldn't be where I am today. And in a sense, everything that I am doing is only a reflection of the way that they raised me. I want to make them proud. I feel like by doing the right thing, by doing what's best for me, and by not settling for anything less, that is the only real form of payment I can give back to them. It just shows that they raised me the right way. Their efforts will pay off because I will continue to strive to make a difference in my life, and in the lives of my family and many others, and in the Native American community.

In addition to my parents, my three grandmas were also extremely important to our development throughout the years. They were always around and always there to help take care of us. I can't explain how much they've done for me and how much they've supported me throughout my life. They would help drive and travel with our AAU team when I was younger. My grandmas would always cook for us and we would spend the night at their houses all the time. It was like having three more moms to help out our family. When we left our hometown and moved to Portland, they made as many trips as possible to come see us and support us with our sport events. The amount of support and love my grandmas have shown is irreplaceable and immeasurable. They helped raise me and they've influenced me to want to be better and strive to do my best in everything I come across. I know without them I wouldn't be where I am or who I am today. I cannot thank them enough for their unconditional love and never-ending support.

I've always been close to my siblings as well, and they are my pride and joy. We have always been inseparable and I love them all so much. Shae, who is my oldest brother, is one of the most intelligent people I know. I have the utmost respect for him and think so highly of him.

I admire his natural talent in sports and his artistic ability. Shoni, my older sister, was always my biggest role model growing up. She is fearless and has true indestructible confidence. We are only a year-and-a-half apart in age so we have shared about every life experience together – both the good and the bad, which is one reason we have always been so close. Job, the next oldest after me, is probably the biggest-hearted person I've ever met. I love how much he loves and genuinely cares for others -- and he's extremely witty and smart. I admire him because I think he has a unique way of understanding all people. Milan, my younger sister, is the most gorgeous girl I know. On top of that, she is so very creative, a natural entertainer, and one of the funniest people I've ever met. She's adaptable to anything and knows how to make the most and best of any situation. Mick is the mysterious brother. He's extremely handsome and has the heart of a lion, but he likes to try and hide that side of himself. He's also a very hard worker. He knows what it takes to accomplish his goals and he won't settle for anything less than his best effort. Saint is like my best friend. He is extremely mature, and has a great personality. He knows how to get along with anyone of any age, and he never fails to amaze me. And finally there is Sun, the baby of the family. He is extremely smart. And of course, he can be a handful, but he is the biggest sweetheart you can ever imagine.

I also have two cousins who grew up with us – Cicily and Isaiah – whom I consider siblings as well. Cicily is extremely funny and one of the most selfless people I know. We laugh together about everything and have ever since we were very young. I love her because her goodness and kind heart keep me humble. Isaiah is close in age to me and we attended school together for many years. He is just like a brother to me. I admire him because he is brutally honest and realistic about everything.

And finally there is Sam. Sam is my best friend and has been since the third grade. She is the most caring person I've met when it comes to not asking or wanting anything in return. She is a great listener and supports my family and me like we were her own.

I am eternally grateful for these remarkable people and the many, many others who have been a part of my life. They all have taught me lessons which have helped me grow and learn as an individual. They've helped me become the person that I am today, and I am very blessed to have these people play important roles in my life. Each and every one of them will always hold a special place in my heart.

PART 1: MY STORY

SPORTS

My parents recognized the power and value of sports for my siblings and me, and started us all in sports at young ages. Our lives have mostly revolved around sports, but they've always been kept in balance and perspective as well. My parents have utilized sports to teach us, as well as every player they've ever coached, the valuable life lessons that we would need to succeed in the real world.

I was four years old when I played basketball for the first time. I played in one of our reservation's local tournaments. Shoni was on my team, and my parents were our coaches. I remember the fun atmosphere, and the roles Shoni and I had on the court were very similar to roles we would have throughout our college careers. She did a lot of the scoring, and I would come in as the defender. My family likes to call me the "secret weapon" because most of the time no one really expects me to do some of the things I do on the basketball court due to my height and size. I was always the smallest player on the court, but that never seemed to affect my fight or my effort. When I was young I remember being on the court feeling nothing but carefree and happy. And playing basketball seemed to come very naturally to me. I loved playing with my sister, my other family members, and my friends. In short, basketball was always just so much fun to me.

Although basketball was the most significant sport in my life and took up the most time, I also participated in many other sports and activities at an early age including softball, cross country, volleyball, and track. My mom was a runner and she used to take all of us jogging with her, and that started my enjoyment of running. I started formally competing in cross country when I was in third grade. I would run with Shoni, Cicily, and their entire middle school team. I was used to participating in sports with kids older than I was and it all felt so natural to me. I'm not sure why but I really enjoyed the challenge of competing with those with more experience than myself. I also played Little League softball in the town of Pendleton, which was about fifteen minutes from our house on the reservation. I enjoyed softball and was able to play on all-star teams and compete in state tournaments. I was always pretty fast, and I really enjoyed running track as well. I participated in the annual Hershey's Track meet and did well, and even made it to the national level in Hershey, Pennsylvania one year. However, volleyball was hands-down my favorite sport when I was younger. Some may find this odd as I attended college on a basketball scholarship but volleyball came the most naturally to me and I simply had more fun playing it than any other sport.

All of these other sports were very important to me growing up, but without a doubt basketball had the biggest impact on my life – and ultimately had the biggest impact on my entire family. When I was in third grade, my parents made a life-changing and important decision for all of us. They decided to start their own AAU program for Shoni and me. It was called American Horse, and it was a big sacrifice for them. In other sports, there always seemed to be underlying factors holding us back from reaching our full potential. However, with American Horse my parents had control over decisions and a chance to control our destiny – which would eventually pay off.

American Horse was truly our program. My mom and grandma came up with the name, and my grandma designed the logo. We couldn't afford real uniforms, and many of our players didn't even own basketball shoes. We wore t-shirts and non-matching shorts, but none of us seemed to care about those things. We were happy just to be out there and to have the opportunity to play basketball. I remember the other teams looked down on us and doubted our ability prior to games. We didn't have tall players or fancy uniforms, but we did have heart and passion. As usual, I was the smallest player on the team. And as usual, that didn't bother me one bit. When we first started playing we lost a lot of games to bigger, better, and stronger teams, but as we started practicing that quickly changed. We began to win games, and that turned into us not settling for anything less than victories. Eventually, we began to beat anyone and everyone we faced.

I think a lot of our individual and team improvement came from the fact that our parents would take the time out of their lives and allow us to practice almost every single day. We would literally do the same exact drills and style of practices day in and day out. We performed the same shooting drills, the same defensive drills, the same rebounding drills, and the same ball handling drills. We also did a lot of running. Boy, did we do a lot of running. To many, running may seem like a punishment, but my Mom found a way to make it more interesting and fun. By making us record our times and compete against ourselves and each other, she made it seem more like a fun challenge to get better rather than a punishment or a conditioning tool. Those same drills and practice styles would eventually be the same ones my parents would use for us all the way through high school.

The few years that we had this team were some of the most memorable years of my life. The experience with American Horse was really the first time I began to have a legitimate relationship with my mom and dad as coaches. My mom's coaching style is very strict and demanding, but also very effective. Her style of coaching is the exact reason why my team, my sister, and I were able to develop like we did. There is no denying that my mom's style was tough, but I wouldn't have wanted it any other way. She knows how to get the best out of every single person, and that's what she has done since day one of her coaching career. I've seen her make terrible players into effective role players and even into all-stars on the court over and over again.

However, I believe the real reason my mom is so well respected and successful as a coach is because she truly cares about her players off the court as much as she does on the court. Of course she was competitive and wanted us to win games, but it was more important to her to help us win at life. She wasn't only our coach, but she was a caring mother figure to all of her players. She would teach our entire American Horse team the same life lessons that she would teach my siblings and me at home. This is just another reason why I have so much respect for her. And, in my opinion, she's the reason why my sister and I, along with every young girl on our team, were able to grow into righteous and successful young women.

In addition to their role as coaches, my parents and my grandmas were also our team's transportation. During any given tournament, my parents would be responsible for transporting my entire family – all 12-15 of us – plus the 10-12 Native American girls on the team – all in an effort to allow us the opportunity to play basketball and do something positive with our lives. We would travel to different cities in two or three cars, and we would all find a way to share three or four hotel rooms. It was during these trips that my parents would also take us on field trips to places that may seem insignificant — such as Chuck E. Cheese, the movies and amusement parks — but looking back these had a positive impact on me and helped our family and team grow closer. I've realized as I've become older that these memories were actually experiences that were helping us grow into the people we were meant to be, and they have not only greatly impacted my life, but the lives of many others as well. They truly helped lay a foundation and set a path for us to be successful and honorable individuals. My parents were forced to sacrifice in order to give my siblings and me the opportunities to play sports and learn the valuable life lessons that they knew would positively shape us for the rest of our lives. They pushed us all to be the best we could be in every possible way through sports, which would also translate into all other areas of our lives. My parents were more than basketball coaches, they were life coaches. All of the players that they coached on that American Horse team graduated from high school, a majority went on to college, and all were successful within their own rights.

As I've mentioned, my parents sacrificed a lot for all of our sakes in order to allow us to participate in sports and learn these important lessons. They had seven kids of their own to raise, yet they took on the challenge of allowing even more people into our lives. It's because of commitments such as this that my life has turned out the way it has. My parents took the time to care and provide for my siblings and me, which gave me the opportunity to play sports. They raised me in a way that taught me the right values that are necessary when it comes to hard work and meaningful achievements. My parents taught me the difference between what is important and what is not. They taught me what to value and how to handle different situations that life may throw at me. And they used sports as the tool to implement all of these lessons into our lives.

I've used the same experiences and lessons as guidelines throughout my entire life. The way my parents coached us is still with me today. The things they taught me on and off the court are still significant, even decades later. I think that shows that what they were teaching me, and so many others, were real-life skills that would always remain relevant. Everything they taught me made me want to be the best I could be as an individual and to work for the greater good. It all goes back to just living a good, happy, positive, and successful life. All of that is still important in my everyday life today.

PART 1: MY STORY

TRANSITION YEARS

My early years were filled with school, family, sports and fun, and I considered myself a normal Native American girl growing up on a reservation. However, as I grew into my middle and high school years I had many life-changing events occur. In their own way, each of these contributed to my overall ability to succeed well into the future. Although I didn't realize it at the time, my parents were implementing a very well-thought-out plan that ultimately was put into place in order for me and my siblings to have the best possible opportunities. Looking back, some of the decisions they made for us were risky, but I think my parents knew that the possible benefits far outweighed the risks that were involved.

During the summer between my seventh and eighth grade years with the help of my parents I made the decision to skip the eighth grade. I wanted the opportunity to play high school basketball for an extra year with my sister Shoni. The school administration advised my parents and me not to do this as they felt I wasn't ready academically, and also thought it would be too big of a challenge in other respects. My parents and I felt strongly that skipping the grade was the right thing to do, and we followed our gut instincts against the advice of the administration. Looking back, I always valued my grades and education but the fact that people were doubting my ability only made me want to work that much harder to do well in school.

My freshman year we attended Hermiston High School, and it was about forty-five minutes from our house on the reservation. Hermiston was actually the rival school of Pendleton High School, which was at the time the closest high school to our reservation and typically the one most people from my reservation attended. The decision to bypass Pendleton High School in order to attend the rival Hermiston did not sit well with many people in Pendleton. We were routinely called traitors and shunned in other ways by many individuals. However, my parents made that school decision based upon what they felt was in our best interests, and they knew that we were well prepared for any negativity that may come our way from the decision. My family also sacrificed tremendously to allow us to attend school in Hermiston. My parents and my grandmas committed to taking turns to drive us (Shoni, Cicily, Isaiah, Sam, and me) forty-five minutes each way at least twice per day because none of us had a license at the time. This is just another example of how much sacrifice my family demonstrated during these years for the benefit of our education, our athletics, and most important our future.

Being a shy and introverted thirteen-year-old who had just skipped ahead one year, my freshman year of high school was quite an experience. I felt like I had no problem making friends or adjusting socially, which was another credit to my parents for preparing me for situations like that. I made the cross country varsity team, and the junior varsity and varsity basketball teams. I was blessed to have special coaches in both of these sports who helped me excel in each one, but who also challenged me in certain ways, which helped me grow into a responsible teenager.

I also had no problem adjusting to the academics of high school, and I finished that year with a 3.9 grade point average. I feel like that entire year was a great example of how you can succeed in spite of the fact there are people out there who are going to doubt you. I was taught that there will be doubters in my life, as there are in everyone's lives, but also I was taught to believe in my own abilities. I worked hard, and was purposeful in my efforts to do the best that I could possibly do both athletically and academically.

That year wasn't always easy though and it definitely had its ups and downs. There were times we had to deal with unfairness because people didn't understand our family's lifestyle. I had to deal with what I considered an unfair lack of playing time for the first time in my life, as I usually was only put in varsity games for thirty seconds or a couple of minutes at the end of games. As a thirteen-year-old it was frustrating, but it only helped me grow and mature. The experience taught me a lot of things, such as the importance of patience and learning to focus on things I actually had control over, as opposed to wasting my time worrying about things I didn't. This was a time that really helped me learn firsthand that not everything is going to go the way you want it to, and you can either let it take over your life or you can focus on the positive and try to make the most of it. As much as I wanted to play and thought I deserved to, going through this experience helped me grow as an individual and helped me keep things in proper perspective. After all, I was thankful that I was the only freshman on the varsity team. If I would've received more varsity playing time that season, I don't think the chain of events that led me to Louisville would've happened. I think it's funny how things work out sometimes.

In an interesting twist, just before my sophomore year of high school my parents moved us to Pendleton High School. This was very odd to me, but I later realized my parents had a bigger plan for us. My mother had applied for coaching jobs outside of our reservation, and my parents felt strongly she would land one soon so it would only be a short period of time before we transferred again. Pendleton was closer and more convenient, and my parents knew it would be much more economical for our family. The Pendleton school experience was cool because I was reunited with many of my old friends from elementary and middle school, but it was very hard on us because, as I mentioned previously, many people thought of us as "traitors" since we attended the rival school the year before. Once again, as a family we tried to make the most of our situation and ignore the negativity.

Because we all knew we would be leaving soon we had to make sure that we did everything right to avoid any hard feelings and unnecessary problems. Therefore we all took care of business and a few months later my whole family and I would end up taking a huge step in transforming our lives.

PART 1: MY STORY

PORTLAND

As I mentioned in my introduction, it is very hard for Native Americans to venture out into the "real world," leave their reservations, and succeed. Reservation life is comfortable for Native Americans, and the culture of reservation life – both the positive and negative aspects – has been deeply embedded in Native American mindsets for generations. For numerous reasons, a cycle of negativity exists within most Native American communities that prevents people from having, pursuing, and even wanting to pursue quality life opportunities. When one looks at the number of Native Americans who grow up on reservations, earn college scholarships, venture away from reservations for school, do well in college, have legitimate opportunities to succeed, and actually succeed outside of reservation life, the numbers are very depressing. It is a very small percentage that are able to do this. Even my mother, whom I've described as one of the most principled, driven, talented, and passionate people I know, was unable to break the cycle and take advantage of opportunities outside of reservation life. No one from my reservation had ever earned a college basketball scholarship, nor made a "big name" for themselves out in the "real world."

It was time for my family to change that.

My Mom made the decision that in order to give us the best possible opportunity to succeed, we needed to move off the reservation. She applied for a coaching position at Franklin High School in Portland, Oregon, and after her interview she was eventually offered the job. When we received the news that she was given the coaching position, we were all initially very excited. I remember I was extremely happy for her, and I realized this meant that I would be given a legitimate opportunity to play with Shoni – which was why I skipped the eighth grade in the first place. But, once the excitement wore off and we actually realized how big of a life changing decision this move would be, most of my family and I became overwhelmed.

I remember my Mom gathering our family in the living room of our Cottonwood Lane house to talk to us about the move. She explained why we were going to do it, and I understood her logic. We all trusted her decision completely. I can't speak for the rest of my family, but I was definitely scared. And I was actually very sad that we were going to be leaving our home on the reservation.

When our family meeting ended, my siblings and I just sat there letting the enormity of the decision sink in. We were all contemplating the big picture, and I think we were all thinking about how much of a challenge this would be for each of us. It's not normal for Native American families to leave the reservation, and my whole family was about to pick up and move three hours away to a big city. I know to a lot of people this may sound like a simple move, but for us it was definitely much more than that. We all took turns shedding tears because of how sad we were that we would have to leave our childhood home behind. For my first fifteen years, reservation life was all that I knew. I loved it, I was comfortable with it, and I didn't want my family to leave the unique atmosphere of a Native American community that we were all accustomed to. It was very hard for me to let go of all that. All the great memories and experiences I had on the reservation constantly ran through my head during the packing process. I really couldn't grasp the fact that we were actually about to make this life-changing move. But, there was no turning back. And I trusted my parents.

About a month later, we arrived at our house in Portland. I was in shock. The house we were moving into was absolutely huge. It had to have been three times the size of our house on the reservation, and it was almost unbelievable to me that it was the house that I would be living in. It sounds funny, but it really seemed like a movie to me as I never imagined our family living in a house like this one. To me, it was the kind of house that rich and affluent people live in -- not some poor Native American family.

As we continued moving into the house and began to settle in, things seemed to go pretty smoothly. It took a lot of getting used to. The atmosphere of the city, the house, the school: everything was much different than life on the reservation. It was all weird to me, but there were a lot of positive aspects too. But at times, the adjustment to being far from home and in a completely different setting and community was definitely overwhelming. For the first few months, I remember being really sad at times because of how much I missed home. But we were moving forward, and it was time to start school -- and basketball.

I remember the first day we met our new teammates. We actually had the opportunity to watch a summer league game of theirs before that school year, and to be honest, at the time they were a terrible team. Their record was approximately four wins and twenty losses. But they were all great girls and there was definitely a good mixture of personalities. We all met in the gymnasium at our school before we enrolled in classes at Franklin, so we all knew nothing of each other. It was at that meeting that I realized everything was going to be fine. Everyone seemed to genuinely and kindly welcome us. My mom was in control of the process, and I knew I'd be given a fair chance on the court and also have the opportunity to play alongside Shoni. I was confident in her as a coach, and knew she could get the most out of our new teammates. I knew that once the girls figured out how my mom operated, everyone would get on board quickly, and we would be successful.

We really began to adjust over the next couple of months. Of course, I still missed the reservation. But, the more accepting people were of us at our new school, the easier and easier things got. There were many key people that really made our transition smooth at Franklin. Two in particular — Franklin's athletic director and school principal — were especially helpful in making us feel comfortable. They had faith in us, were supportive of my mom, saw the changes that she was implementing as big steps forward for the school, and supported us in every way they could. There were times that frustrations would set in for us as a family, but that's normal for any major life-changing move like the one we made. School was going well, basketball was going well, and I was getting used to my new home.

Then one day there was a knock at our door. My Dad answered, and a little kid had dropped off a note for Shoni and me. No one in my family had ever seen the kid before. At first, we assumed it was some type of fan letter, as we would occasionally get those for basketball. However, this was much different. When we opened it, it simply said: "Go back to the f***ing reservation."

We were all really, really confused and somewhat hurt at that point. We had thought everything was going so well, but this letter really put things into perspective that prejudice and racism still very well existed. We never really thought we'd have to deal with that stuff because we were just a Native American family trying to make it in the real world. It's not like we purposefully tried to step on other people's toes or cause problems of any sort. But we also knew that being good people doesn't necessarily mean everyone or everything will be in your favor. Fortunately, through my parents' teachings we were prepared to deal with this type of thing. My parents taught us to ignore the negativity, as there will always be people out there waiting to hurt you. They taught us to look out for ourselves, and realize that some people may try to bring you down. And they taught us the importance of knowing when and how to stand up for ourselves. They made us understand that not everyone is out there trying to do the right and positive thing. Personally, I try not to let that stuff get to me. But, honestly it did. It's not that it made me roll over and fold but it was more a case of reality setting in.

Regardless, we weren't going to let that stop us from achieving our goals. It turned out to be an isolated incident, and we used it positively as motivation more than anything else. We continued moving forward and, as always, I kept my focus on basketball and school.

My sophomore season, we completely turned the program around. We finished 21-3 and went to the state tournament. That's quite a turnaround from the season before when Franklin only won about four games. Further, I had a great season and was named our league's Player-Of-The-Year. This was a big moment for me because in the past I had felt that a lot of people simply saw me as Shoni's little sister. I feel I proved myself that season, and I was very proud that I had earned that award.

In addition to my high school season, this was also the year I joined my AAU team, Reign, which my sister Shoni and my best friend Sam were also a part of. Bryon Sheng, our coach, was extremely helpful and generous to not only me but my entire family. This was a very significant time in my life for many reasons. It allowed me the opportunity to play and compete at a high level and it essentially was a huge reason as to why I was able to be seen by college scouts because we traveled to so many different places. I remember having tournaments in Texas, Indiana, California, and many other states. Additionally, the relationships I built with my teammates were incredible. Each one of them is just like family to me and my family to this day.

The Reign also allowed me the opportunity to experience different parts of the world. My sister and I had the chance to be a part of Candace Parker's Aces All Star team which was an amazing experience for me. This was significant in my life for multiple reasons. We got to spend time in California, meet other top players from across the country, and travel to Tokyo, Japan to compete against great competition. It was the first time I got to travel and experience overseas life. And this was probably the first time in my life I realized that I could do big things with the help of basketball.

The summer after my sophomore season we actually went back to live on the reservation.

My father had kept his job in Pendleton, and it was tough traveling back and forth. My parents were having some money issues, and the new house posed some financial problems as well. However, as always my parents put our best interests first, and sacrificed to allow us to go back to Franklin again the following fall.

During my junior year, our cousins ended up moving to Portland to live with us. So, once again we had twelve to fifteen people living in our house. Even though it was bigger than our reservation house, it began to feel relatively small again because we had so many people living there. It was fun and, of course, crowded, but in a good way because it reminded me of the times spent back on the reservation in our old home.

The good thing about going back to school at Franklin my junior year was that everything was already in place for me both in the classroom, and most important, on the court. My mom would be our coach again, and after the first year with the girls she actually made many of my teammates better players and much more effective on the basketball court. This was both helpful and reassuring to Shoni and me because being a junior and senior in high school we felt like we needed to do some great things since it was our last year together before college. Everything this year was pretty much the same as it was the previous year except for the fact that my two cousins Cicily and Isaiah, and my best friend Sam, ended up moving to Portland. Isaiah and Sam went to school with us at Franklin and Cicily went to a community college nearby. This was also the year that my parents had my youngest brother, Sun, who was born in the spring. But as always we started out the year with our fall sport, cross country, and we all made it to state that year and actually did pretty well.

Then when basketball came around it was go time. I remember thinking that this could be the last year I play basketball with my sister, at least formally, so I knew I had to make the most of it. And we had another solid year. Our record was good and we made it to state, but we ended up losing in the semifinals to a team we knew we were more than capable of beating. However, things just didn't seem to go our way. We were playing fine but the refs didn't seem to be helping our chances. My sister, who hadn't fouled out a single game of her high school career, ended up being fouled out with a few minutes left which would turn out to be similar to the Baylor game during our college years. Then toward the end of the game I fouled out too. The two best players on our team, who had never fouled out, were stuck on the bench and unable to make a difference in the outcome of the game. To me it wasn't a coincidence but everything happens for a reason. I was upset because I knew that was the end of our high school careers together and that wasn't how I expected it to end, but I also knew that it wasn't the end of the world. Life went on and we learned from the experience both mentally and socially. We knew that we could grow as players, and we knew that injustice or discrimination, whether overt and obvious or covert and behind the scenes, still existed and we couldn't control that. The way I saw it was that politics were always involved. The fact was that Franklin, a small public school who hadn't ever made it to the state tournament prior to our years there, and who was now a team with multiple Native Americans and minorities in general, just wasn't a good combination for us. I don't think people expected us to make a name for ourselves by beating predominantly white teams, but we did, which contributed to the negativity we encountered. And that year at the state tournament we were beating one of the top ranked teams, which was a private school, with much better players who were mostly white. I know to some it may sound like an excuse, but to me it wasn't a coincidence the way it ended.

That spring I played softball, and even though I hadn't played since middle school I ended up making varsity and had a lot of fun. Outside of sports and school two of the biggest things I remember from this year were two pretty significant events. One was when my family had to deal with our house being foreclosed. It was just a really frightening time in my life because I knew we weren't made of money but just to see how it affected my parents was something I wasn't used to. It was a huge challenge to deal with but somehow we found a way to get through it. Second was watching my sister and my best friend graduate. It was just a very proud moment for me. I remember watching my older brother, Shae, and my older cousin, Cicily, graduate a few years before but I was much younger then. However, being older and being so close in age to Shoni and Sam made me realize how much closer I was to that point in my life. I remember watching my sister walk up and receive her diploma and I just felt so happy for her. Mostly because I knew she was about to do great things in her life. Graduating high school meant that she would be going off into the bigger world and she would be the first in our family to truly go off to college and make the most of her opportunities. This was also the first time she announced where she would be attending college which had been undecided for quite a while.

The next year, my senior year, was a much different experience for me, but in a good way. This was the year I really got to mature both on and off the court. The previous years I always had Shoni or my family around and they had a huge influence in my school, social, and sports circles. But now it was all me. On the court things were very different. Most of the girls had graduated the year before so it was really just me and a couple of other girls returning. This meant that we would have to start all over with making our team ready to play and win. Again, my mom made them into much better players, but they weren't quite as developed as the girls before them and honestly they really weren't that great so every game was a new challenge for me. I remember my sophomore year when my sister got hurt and sat out for a while and I had to take over but this was different. I can remember being double and triple teamed often but luckily for me it was high school ball and I was just better than other people, so I was able to find ways to be successful. Even though I was always one of the smallest and shortest people on the court that was irrelevant. We still had a winning record and we made it to the playoffs that year, but we ended up losing and missing out on the chance to go back to the state tournament. I finished the season averaging 28.4 points, 9.4 rebounds, 7.3 steals, and 5.6 assists per game and ended my high school career with 1,546 points. Thank goodness these stats were enough to get colleges interested in me.

Again, in the spring time I played softball and I really enjoyed it because I had missed playing it. Softball was like a recreational but still competitive sport for me and I had a couple of friends on the team who made it even more fun. Then that summer when I graduated and decided to join my sister at the University of Louisville life became surreal once again. It was a huge move to Portland but the difference when we made that move was that I was making it with all the members of my family. Now this time, I would be going off to school 2,000 miles away from home and away from my family. I was nervous, scared, and excited. I was happy to be joining my sister once again, and I knew it was going to be very special for her, my family, and myself. But what I didn't know was that my choice to attend college with my sister would actually have a much bigger effect on Native Americans all across the country.

PART 1: MY STORY

LOUISVILLE

Choosing a college was one of the hardest decisions I've ever had to make. I was fortunate to have scholarship opportunities to attend over twenty-five schools such as Columbia, Oregon State, Gonzaga, South Carolina, etc. I had many factors I had to consider, such as if I was going to stay close to home or go far away, whether I was going to attend school with Shoni or not, and whether my primary focus was going to be school or basketball. During my recruiting process I got a lot of offers, but in my opinion I feel like some schools only wanted me because I was Shoni Schimmel's sister. Honestly, that never bothered me. I felt that if she helped get my foot in the door then so be it, because I knew that was all I needed in order to eventually become successful. And regardless of anything I knew that I would be a Division I athlete with the opportunity to earn my college degree. I also had the confidence that if I was given an opportunity I would be able to prove myself on the basketball court.

I ultimately decided to attend the University of Louisville, where Shoni was playing. I am glad I made that decision and it turned out to be pretty perfect for me. At first I was hesitant about going to Louisville. I felt comfort that Shoni was there, but it was still just so far from home and I was unsure about making that big of a move at the age of seventeen. But in the end, I decided on Louisville for a number of reasons. First, it's extremely rare to have the opportunity to play Division I basketball with a sibling – and I didn't want to miss out on that opportunity. In addition, when I made my official visit to Louisville I loved the facilities that they had to offer. I felt comfortable with the people I met when I was there, and I had respect for the coaching staff and the overall direction of the school and especially the basketball program.

Once I realized everything that the University of Louisville had to offer, I felt even more appreciative of the opportunity to attend. The athletic department is one of the best in the country. UofL's athletic director, Tom Jurich, is one of the best in the business. What he has created over his years at Louisville is incredible. UofL is a sports powerhouse and there was no better time to be a part of Louisville sports than during the time I attended. All of the sports at Louisville were successful, not just one. Louisville is known across the country for their athletics, and I was proud to represent them and the women's basketball program.

On top of that, there are few professional sports teams in the city of Louisville, which means all of the fans were focused on UofL's athletics. The University of Louisville fan support was one of the things I appreciated most during the years I played. It didn't matter where I went, people knew who I was simply because I played basketball for the University of Louisville. Our fans showed up strong for every home game and even many away games, and we ranked in the top three teams in national attendance in each of my years there. The fans were always very knowledgeable, supportive, and very enthusiastic about Louisville athletics. And I felt even more grateful after playing away games and seeing what the "normal" level of support was for most other colleges. The genuine dedication and consistency of support from our fans was simply amazing, and I am so thankful to have experienced that.

Additionally, the University of Louisville was very strong academically, and that was another factor in my decision to attend school there. Fortunately the coaches and administration valued grades and academics just as much as athletic success. Good grades have always been a priority for me, but the fact that we had the available resources made it that much easier to be successful when it came to school.

We had very good academic advisors who were very valuable to my teammates and me, who made sure we were on track to be academically eligible and more important on track to graduate.

The city was also perfect for a college student. It wasn't too big, and it wasn't too small. And the campus was perfect as well. UofL had beautiful sports fields and facilities, and everything was within a ten-minute walk. Having everything on campus within walking distance actually made a very big difference in my college experience. I know many schools weren't set up like this, but it made life much easier especially since I didn't have a car all four years.

And of course there were my coaches. Coach Jeff Walz had built the women's program into a consistent national contender, and I was proud to be a part of that. I am not going to lie: there were some times that I really didn't see eye to eye with the coaching staff, especially during my freshman year. But looking back I couldn't be more thankful to have had the coaches I did. They really helped me grow as a person, and I'm grateful for the way they challenged me in ways both good and bad, which made me grow into a stronger individual on and off the court. The relationships I had with them were crucial to my success and I'm thankful for everything they did for me during my years at UofL.

Finally, there are my teammates- Tia, Asia, Nita, Shelby, Mo, Sheronne, Shawnta', Sara, Bria, Megan, Cortnee, Emmonnie, Arica, Myisha, Mariya, Ari, Syd, Monny, Starr, and Shoni. I made friendships with them that I'll always be thankful for. My teammates were just like my sisters, and I love and care for each and every one of them. All of the laughs and inside jokes we had together, all of the practices, and just all of the time we spent together exposed me to so many different relationships and experiences. Of course we had ups and downs together, but the ups and downs were all just a part of the process that we were going through together as Division I student-athletes. And even though it was never perfect I wouldn't have changed a thing about what we all experienced together. My friendships with my teammates helped me grow as a person, helped me appreciate others more, and helped me learn many new things. I already miss them like crazy. Even though we may all be in different places now, I know someday we'll be reunited because we promised to invite each other to all of our weddings and baby showers. (PS: I'm still holding all of you to that.)

Simply stated, playing at the University of Louisville was a great experience for me. The support I received while there was truly amazing. A perfect example of this support is the Native American appreciation night that the university arranged for us. This event gave us a chance to show our gratitude and meet many of the Native Americans that had previously given my sister and me support in our basketball careers. The athletic department, marketing department, our coaches, and staff were all key in helping make this a reality. The turnout was overwhelming, but in the best way possible and during the three-hour autograph session following the game, many people shared their stories of traveling and driving hours upon hours just to see us play. The official attendance was announced at over 22,000 for that game. Even though we routinely drew Native American fans during away games, I never imagined that we would have an additional 12,000 fans who were predominantly Native American attend that game at the KFC Yum! Center to show their support for Shoni and me. The atmosphere was incredible that night. From the traditional Native American songs and dances performed at half time, to the hundreds of creative signs dedicated to us throughout the venue, the night was truly a celebration and display of Native American pride.

Looking back on each of my four years at the University Louisville, it's amazing to see the transformation that occurred each year, and I was definitely an entirely different person after my senior year than as a freshman first coming into college.

My freshman year didn't go very well for me. I was quiet, shy, and hardly talked unless it was necessary. On the court, I didn't feel that I was getting a fair opportunity and I thought I deserved to play more. I barely played most games, and there were some games that I didn't play at all. But I realized years later that what happened during my freshman year happened for a reason and it taught me some valuable lessons. To be honest, as much as I liked the University, I sincerely hated being away at school for much of my freshman year. I had the worst possible attitude during that time. And I was extremely unhappy being away from my family. I went home that summer after my freshman year and I didn't want to go back. I remember sitting at my grandma's house just crying and trying to figure out what I would do next. I decided I didn't want to go through any of that again, so I called Coach Walz and told him that I didn't want to come back. However, for some reason I decided to give it another try and ended up booking a flight back to Louisville. When I got back to school, I had a meeting with Coach Walz and we had a really good and helpful talk. He helped me see that I had two options. Either I could transfer to a school closer to home, or I could stay at UofL, put two feet in, and buy into everything at Louisville in every possible way. I chose the latter route and I'm very glad that I did. I may not have known it at the time but it was honestly a life-changing decision for me.

I could've chosen to take the easy route and go back home. By making the tougher decision and choosing to change my attitude and whatever else was in my control, my life completely changed for the better. My team went to the Final Four and played in the National Championship game that next season. I did very well in school and won the Elite 89 award at the Final Four for having the top grade-point-average for any of the Final Four participants. Shoni and I were featured in Sports Illustrated for our accomplishments. I was also named as one of *Glamour* Magazine's Top 10 College Women. The moral of the story is I didn't take the easy way out of simply quitting and going back home. I made a choice to better myself and to persevere, and as I said it was truly a life changing and amazing transformation for me. I became much more content with my life and made the most of everything that I needed to be focused on. Even more important I began to see people, situations, and everything else differently. My attitude towards things just changed and that's what really made the difference for me. I was in the same place with most of the same people with the same situations. It was just I who decided to change. Once I started to mature, I started seeing the good in everything and great things happened for me. The fact that I started to really grow up made it so I could reflect on myself and realize what I could change in order to make my situation better. I stopped blaming everyone and everything else and decided to focus on the things I had control over rather than the things I couldn't control. And after I did that everything in my life began to fall into place.

My junior year was a solid one. I remember we had a lot of returning players from the year before and that we were all great players and highly experienced. This was the year we were determined to make it back to the Final Four. Overall, it was a successful year but I think all of us were disappointed in the outcome. The one game I'll always remember from this year was the Elite Eight game against Maryland. We made an incredible comeback but came up short. Despite the basketball outcome this was another year that Shoni and I continued to be influential and role models to the Native American community. We were featured on HBO's Real Sports with Bryant Gumbel which was another huge honor to use our success as an example for others to follow, strive for, and surpass. Yet again, this was another very significant thing in my life because I never imagined I would have these types of opportunities and success.

In addition, I had another life- changing moment during my junior year of college. And to be honest I was hesitant about sharing this part of my life, but I know that everybody goes through similar experiences and I wanted people to realize that I am human and just like they do, I have to deal with personal obstacles as well. During the second semester, I lost the friendship of one of the most significant people in my life at that time. My life completely got turned upside down. It was a situation like many people go through, when you think you're in love but you later realize that you were just young and may not have known what was best for you. I actually wasn't even supposed to have a boyfriend, but I did for seven years, and he really was my best friend. We broke up, and I thought it was the end of the world. I skipped classes. I hardly left my room. I barely talked to anyone. I did terribly in school. I pretty much stopped doing everything except for playing basketball. But once I got myself together, I finally realized how much better off I was without that relationship. And most important I bounced back from it all and ended up becoming a much better me than I ever was before. I don't blame anyone for the outcome of the situation, but more important I came to grips that some things just aren't meant to be. I realized that it all happened for a reason – just like all experiences do. This particular experience taught me to grow as an individual and ever since then my life was completely different. I became a completely better person. I became much more focused on my personal goals and the greater good, and I became much happier. I learned a lot from this rough time in my life. I felt like it was a moment that was meant to make me crash so that I could begin to build my life into what it was truly meant to be. It allowed me to change my priorities and keep my focus on my goals. During the time I was going through this challenge, I never would've thought I'd ever view it as a positive. But that's the lesson here – sometimes you have to step back and look at things from a different perspective. I just learned a lot from this experience, and even though it wasn't easy to deal with I'm thankful for it. It sincerely helped me grow and mature into a young woman, the type of woman I've always strived to be.

My senior year at UofL was similar to my senior year in high school when Shoni left to go off to college. Except this time, she left to be a professional athlete. I felt like it was another opportunity in my life for me to grow on and off the court and to show everybody the things that they didn't necessarily see when we were together. Surprisingly, my senior year was my favorite one. I felt like everything was finally in place. I had a solid relationship with my coaches. I got along great with every single one of my teammates. And most importantly I was a leader. My first three years of college I was well aware that I was a role player but my senior year was just different. I may not have scored all the points or had the leading stats but I was whatever my team needed me to be in order for us to be successful. I'll always remember the South Florida game to go to the Sweet Sixteen. I feel like this was the game everything I had done and worked for all came together. In reflection, I feel like this game showed my heart, my work ethic, and determination to be successful despite what odds were against me. I was honestly really proud of myself. And I mentioned that I wasn't a stat leader; however, that night I happened to lead in every category- points, rebounds, assists, and steals. I usually don't like to brag but that game was that significant to me because I helped my team get a huge win and it meant a lot to so many different people. Nobody expected us to do well that year and I guess you could say we were a little underrated. This was the first year ever we were a part of the ACC which is the most powerful conference in women's basketball and we finished third place both in the regular season and in the conference tournament. In addition to that my team made it to the Sweet Sixteen. Of course, we all would've liked to be in the Final Four but everything happens for a reason and I couldn't be more proud of my team. We didn't have the best players but we found a way to win and I'll always cherish the memories and relationships I made my senior year at Louisville.

Finally, just the fact that I got to experience college with my sister was truly a blessing. Of course it had its ups and downs but I am beyond thankful to have had the opportunity to do that. It's very rare for siblings of any background to do this but for two Native American women to attend college together, graduate from college, and be successful on the basketball court was an amazing experience. And I've realized as time has developed that it's all much bigger than just Shoni and me and our family. All of this has and will continue to impact many people across the country. I'm thankful that Coach Walz gave us the chance and believed in us.

PART 1: MY STORY

BAYLOR

People often ask me what is the most memorable game I've ever played in. I've been fortunate to have the opportunities to experience many special games over the years. Playing against UConn in the 2013 national championship was special, despite losing the game. Beating the University of Tennessee to go to the Final Four that same season, as well as winning against a great California team to get to the championship game, were both extremely memorable experiences as well. I also remember certain games where I had big and significant personal contributions such as the game I scored 51 points in high school against Century in Oregon. During my sophomore year in college against Texas A&M I had a big steal and a layup to seal a win at the end of the game at the KFC Yum! Center. I remember a great game against Oklahoma where I scored four key points quickly at the end of the game to send the game into overtime, which we eventually ended up winning in double overtime. Another one that stands out to me was when we played Florida State during my junior year of college, and I had yet another big steal at the end and a layup to win the game. I could go on and on about significant memories and significant games. I've been blessed to be able to play a part in so many over the years and with some great teammates.

However, by far the most memorable game I've ever been a part of was the Baylor game of 2013. As I mentioned in the introduction, Baylor was widely considered one of the better teams of all time. They were the overall number one seed of the tournament, and overwhelming favorites to win the championship. They were the defending national champions, and featured 6'8" star Brittney Griner, whom many have considered the top female player of all time. Once again, they were 27-point favorites over us that night.

I clearly remember the day that they announced the NCAA® seedings and brackets. I was at the KFC Yum! Center for the selection show with our team and fans. Shoni was just getting out of class so she wasn't with us yet when the pairings were announced. She saw them and immediately texted me predicting that we were going to face Baylor in the third round — and that we were going to beat them. I thought she was crazy at that moment. I thought there was no way we were going to beat the best team in the country and the number one overall seed. But the more and more I talked about it with Shoni, the more I thought it really could happen. She had no doubt that we were going to face them and beat them.

We won the first two rounds of the tournament handily, beating good Middle Tennessee and Purdue teams at home in Louisville. We were playing well and playing together as a team. Baylor dominated their first two opponents as well, which set up the matchup in Oklahoma City that we all were waiting for.

Over the course of the days leading up to that big game, the talks and confidence that started between Shoni and me had spread to our teammates. The closer it got to the game, the more certain I was that we were going to win. By this time, everybody, including the coaches, were on the same page, and we all shared the same confidence and certainty that we could pull off the upset. Going into the game, we were aware that we may have been the only ones who believed we could do it, but that didn't matter to us because we knew the outcome was in our hands and we knew we could win.

When my parents were driving to Oklahoma City to watch us play, they started talking about the game themselves. We had already told them outright that we were going to win. My mom told my dad that if we were to win the game, she would marry him. My dad questioned it and had to make sure that she was serious – and she was. He made the comment that the game was being played on Easter Sunday, and that's a day miracles happen. I can't help but to think that game and that win were both just meant to happen for my family.

The day of the game just felt different. I could sense this was going to be a special day.

During a pregame meeting, Coach Walz arranged for us to watch *Survive and Advance*, a documentary about the 1982 North Carolina State Wolfpack and their underdog run to the national championship. Interestingly enough, it was produced by Jon Hock, who produced our family's *Off the Rez* documentary and who is now a very special friend to our family. After the video, Coach Walz had Charles Whittenburg, captain of that North Carolina State team, call us to give us some inspirational words of encouragement before the game. He told us that we had the tools to win the game, and it was up to us to execute and do what we needed to do. His message was that if we believed in our teammates and ourselves, anything was possible. He fired us up even more than we already were, emphasizing the message that it was us against the world, David vs. Goliath.

Just before we took the court for our shoot-around, we were able to talk briefly to our parents. They told us about the bet and how they would be getting married if we won.
As if we weren't already motivated enough, this only inspired us more.

As game time approached and we took the court for warm-ups, I remember the arena being packed with fans from the different teams. There were a lot of Native Americans there for us, as well as numerous UofL fans, including most of our families. The arena was loud, and you could sense the excitement of the NCAA® tournament in the air. ESPN and countless other media outlets were there to cover this Sweet 16 matchup, and in hindsight it was the perfect stage for arguably the biggest upset in the history of NCAA® Women's Basketball.

My team's sense of watching Baylor take the court that day and warm up was that they felt they were invincible and thought they were going to dominate us. That was understandable to me based on everything they had already accomplished up to that point. However, my team was so focused that day that we didn't let it bother us. If anything, it made us want to win that much more. Of course we were aware that they were considered a powerhouse. I wasn't the least bit nervous. I knew Shoni and my teammates were prepared and ready as well. And nothing could break our focus. We didn't think twice about Baylor's status, who they were, what their record was, what players they had, or how many consecutive games they had won. We were just going to play the game that day. I feel like a lot of people fold under pressure, but I feel our whole team was determined and convinced that it was our game going into it, and that we were going to win. It probably sounds crazy to the rest of the world, but that was our mindset.

Our coaches' game plan for us was very simple that day. We were going to try and limit Brittney Griner's touches by double-teaming her defensively. We were going to shoot a lot of threes, and we knew there was no reason anyone should get a dunk on us.

When the game started, everything seemed to go our way. We were executing our coaches' game plan to perfection. We were playing great defense. We were limiting Griner's touches. We were outhustling them. And we were hitting three-pointers. Boy were we hitting three-pointers.

As we built a lead early on, it only gave us more and more confidence. We continued to feed off of that energy, and our lead continued to grow. We led by as much as 19 points. It was truly our team playing as a team and everyone was contributing. Nita Slaughter was shooting the lights out. Sara Hammond hit a big step-back three in Griner's face. I hit two three-pointers. Sheronne Vails even hit a three, and everyone was playing great defense. Of course, Shoni was doing her thing: hitting tough shots, making big time plays, and leading our team in the biggest game of our lives.

I approached the game as I would any other one. I knew my role was to be the first off the bench, take care of the ball, bring defensive energy, and control the tempo of the game. My team was already doing really well before I entered the game, so my focus was to continue that momentum.

I remember playing as hard as I possibly could, and toward the end I was beyond exhausted. In the second half, I even asked for a breather, which seems silly and was definitely out of character for me. After Coach Walz told me no, I had to find it within myself to fight through my exhaustion until the next timeout.

We were playing hard, and we were playing to win. There are probably a million different perspectives on this game, and I know some people may have seen it differently, but to us we were just playing basketball.

We weren't trying to foul intentionally or do anything unsportsman-like, we were just trying to win the game.

When we had the lead on Baylor, I could sense they weren't used to being in that position and a sense of panic was setting in. Our magic continued throughout the game and we held a fourteen point lead with 9:56 left to go. Then there was a signature moment that occurred for my team, my family, and for Native Americans everywhere.

I remember getting a big rebound, throwing an outlet pass to my sister on the right side of the court, and watching her take off. Shoni changed directions with a behind-the-back dribble, and all that stood between her and the basket was 6'8" Brittney Griner – the NCAA® all-time leader in blocked shots. With a move I've seen Shoni practice since we were little, she drove directly at Griner, twisted in mid-air, and shot a no-looker as she was fouled. Shoni went down on the ground, and the ball went in. She immediately jumped back up with a lot of emotion. After the ball went in, I sprinted to celebrate with my sister the biggest play of her college career. In that moment, I really couldn't help but smirk at the fact that my sister had just done that. It's not that I hadn't seen her do it before, but it was the fact that it was the biggest game of our lives and she was incorporating something she had practiced since we were little. Everyone was just in awe of that play and that shot. And even though I was extremely excited in the moment, after celebrating it I was just thinking that that is my sister to a tee. I've seen her practice those shots, and I've seen her make trick plays like that throughout our entire basketball careers. I felt a mixture of "wow, that really just happened," but also I was not the least bit surprised.

That moment summed up the entire game.

We continued to storm forward after that and kept our momentum going. I never gave much thought to Baylor making a comeback as we were playing at such a high level and had such a big lead, but they were the overall #1 seed for a reason. Baylor did make a remarkable comeback. As the final minutes drew near, we were in foul trouble. For the first time in her college career, Shoni fouled out with four minutes left to play. And we lost two other starters – Bria Smith and Sara Hammond. Shoni had fouled out in our state tournament in high school in a similar scenario, and I couldn't help but to think back to that game and how we lost that one. I was determined that the outcome was going to be different this time.

I was completely exhausted, but was able to keep fighting for and with my teammates. While holding on to a slim lead at the time, I stole the ball from their point guard with about one minute left to play, and I thought that play may have secured the win for us, but I was wrong. Baylor kept fighting, we made a couple of mistakes, and they took a one-point lead with 7 seconds left to play.

Monique Reid, a fifth year senior, took an inbounds pass and drove the length of the court as the clock was winding down. She was fouled by Baylor as she attempted a layup, and was put at the free throw line with a chance to win, tie, or lose the game for us. She came through under pressure and hit both free throws to give us the lead. As Baylor's last-second shot missed, our celebration was on.

When we won all I felt was pure happiness. Throughout my whole life and my whole career I've played in big games before, but winning this one was much bigger than winning any other basketball game. And I understood that. Being able to share that moment with my sister, and having my parents and siblings there, meant everything to me - and made it 10 times better.

After the game ended and after our initial celebration, an ESPN crew asked to interview me. It suddenly hit me and I remembered that this win meant that my parents would be getting married now. I completely ignored the television cameras and found my parents in the stands, and kept pointing to my ring finger signaling to them my excitement. It's funny; I think most people who saw me do that thought I was signaling about some type of championship ring. That definitely wasn't the case. And my parents knew exactly what I was saying.

The next day my parents were married at the courthouse in Oklahoma City.

My parents had been together for over 25 years, and had always sacrificed their time, money, and energy for us in order to maximize our basketball opportunities. They were always so focused on providing for us that they put their own wants, needs and interests on hold. In other words, they always put their kids first, and I found it ironic that the kids they sacrificed for were ultimately the reason they finally got married.

Over the years, we had played countless games as underdogs. It seems we were underdogs in other areas of life as well. In the past, it always felt like we came up short, but the outcome of this game showed that we had it in us all along. In previous moments of our sport careers, it often felt like the world was against us, and you could usually feel the unfairness whether it was bad calls, unruly opposing fans, or other unjust circumstances. But the result of this game was different. It was perfect.

Thinking back to when I first began playing basketball, it felt like all of the work, time and dedication I committed to it over the years all paid off during that game. And it just so happened to be the biggest stage of our lives. The fact that all of the odds were against us, the fact that many people doubted us… somehow we managed to overcome all of the obstacles by winning that game. We made a difference. It was much more than just a basketball win; it was a huge win for the history of women's basketball. It was also a huge win for the University of Louisville. Obviously it was a huge win for my family and me. And additionally it was a huge win for Native Americans everywhere. With all of that it is definitely something that people will always remember.

After playing in that game, to this day I can't help but sit back and reflect about where I came from, where I started, and how I played at the highest level against the best teams in the country -- alongside my sister. And we were successful. I strongly believe that everything happens for a reason, and I felt like the Baylor experience was one of those times. As I've mentioned, I almost didn't return to Louisville after my freshman season. Without returning, I wouldn't have experienced that win, I wouldn't be writing this book, and my parents wouldn't be married today. Who says the choices we make today don't affect what we do in the future?

THE ESPYS

After the Baylor win, my teammates and I were nominated for an ESPY award for the year's biggest upset. I was honored to be able to attend the ceremony along with my sister and three of my teammates. The ESPY experience was another example of something I would've never dreamed I'd be participating in. It was definitely one of the most memorable experiences of my life. Growing up, I watched the ESPYs on television but never pictured myself there.

Being around all of the celebrities was unbelievable. I was surrounded by some of the biggest stars in sports and entertainment. We met and saw celebrities such as Dwyane Wade, LeBron James, Mike Epps, Gabrielle Union, John Wall, Michael Phelps, Ray Lewis, Ray Allen, Selena Gomez, Robin Roberts, P Diddy, and many others. It was a really cool experience. One of the first people we met was one of our idols growing up, Lisa Leslie. And she actually knew who we were. It was quite surreal. Having someone on her level know who we were was amazing. I will always remember Robin Roberts and her speech that she gave about her illness. It was very touching. And I'll remember just in general how exciting it was to be there. The whole experience was fascinating, and it's completely different than when you watch it on TV. Actually being a part of it is very special. The fact that I got to share it with my sister made it that much better. How many people can say they played basketball at the highest level with their sibling, then on top of that you get to share that type of experience? It's really rare and it makes me appreciate it even more.

When our category was announced, I thought we would win hands-down because in my opinion there had never been a bigger upset in the NCAA® tournament. Unfortunately, that wasn't the case and we didn't win. I was disappointed, but at the same time I was just happy we won the game and were nominated for the award. And I was thankful to get to live that memorable experience of attending the ESPYs.

Going through the whole process of getting dressed, going on the red carpet, being surrounded by pro athletes and entertainers, was all like a dream. Being there made me feel like everything in my past had led up to this moment. It was an honor to be nominated and invited to the ESPYs, and I also felt that all of my hard work was being rewarded once again. My mom always preached to us that if you work hard and keep your intentions good, then all of that good will come back to you. This was one of those moments. It will be an experience that I will remember and cherish for the rest of my life.

ELITE 89

The Elite 89 award is presented to the participant who has the top grade-point average in each of the NCAA®'s 89 different sports. It also has to be awarded to someone who has been actively participating in their respective sport who then advances to the championships. It is a very prestigious award and is an extremely high honor.

In 2013 at the Final Four in New Orleans, we were leaving practice at the Superdome and Coach Walz had informed me that I would be receiving the NCAA® Elite 89 award for having the highest grade point average among the competing teams. When he told me that, I was really happy and very proud of myself, because all of my hard work in the classroom was once again paying off, and now this time it was on an even bigger stage than ever before. I am the only one in the whole country from women's Division I basketball that can say that for that year. To some this may not seem like a huge accomplishment but for a young Native American female, being honored for academics in addition to basketball success, I felt more than accomplished. I feel very proud of the fact that I have the values of hard work and success instilled in me. Additionally education has always been so important to me, and I always try to stress the importance of education to others whenever I can. I feel like being able to receive that award was kind of perfect because it shows a reflection of hard work and versatility which have been very significant in my life since I was a young girl.

I remember being announced as the winner of the award in between the two Final Four games. I had to walk out in front of everyone, and I was extremely nervous, as I don't like being the center of attention. I think it has a lot to do with the fact that I'm very shy at times. But even though I was very nervous, I was really proud to walk out there and receive the award because it reflects the idea that I've always worked hard in school and grades have always been important to me, but more important it shows that I'm aware of how significant education is to future success after sports. And to just see all of my efforts toward these things to finally be paying off made me feel very accomplished. Although athletic success is significant and highly valued in our society I know ultimately my grades and education will have a much greater impact on my future than basketball ever will.

The fact that we were at the Final Four shows success on the court, and I feel my parents were proud because of that. But receiving an award for taking pride in education, to me shows another way of saying thank you to Mom and Dad for raising me the way you did. Thank you for raising me to have the right priorities and mindset, and for teaching me to not settle for just being good at sports, because there will always be much more than that.

The way I see it is that my decision to skip the 8th grade was life-changing and although years later this may seem irrelevant, it still definitely played a part in me being honored with this award. It's still relevant because although certain people may have doubted me academically at one point in time I used that as fuel to work harder and to achieve success in the classroom and with my education.

During moments like this one I always reflect on the past and just look at how far I've come and I can honestly say that I appreciate every step – good and bad -- of my journey along the way because I know each little thing played a significant role. All the choices I made, valuing grades and education, the standards I had for myself, my conscious decision to always work hard and do my best, and everything else in between had an impact on me and the way my life has turned out.

Being versatile and multidimensional are very good traits to have and good skills to learn. The way I see it, being versatile will give you so much more opportunity and I am very thankful that I was able to be successful both in the classroom and on the court.

In reflection, another thing I always like to consider is how significant my decision to return to Louisville was. I've said before if I hadn't made the decision to go back to school, who is to say I would've received the Elite 89 award. This is an example of how I believe things really do happen for a reason, because after making the choice to go back to school at the University of Louisville I played in a Final Four, I received the Elite 89 award and this was also the year I was first introduced to the *Glamour* opportunity.

GLAMOUR

In 2014, I was humbled to be named one of *Glamour* magazine's Top 10 College Women. The honor is for those who "show campus leadership, scholastic achievement, community involvement, and unique, inspiring goals." I was selected out of a pool of over one thousand applicants. I was able to participate in a panel and celebration in New York City along with the other honorees.

The experience with *Glamour* was unbelievable. I enjoyed every moment of it. At times it made me get out of my comfort zone, and it exposed me to new opportunities that I knew nothing about. The other nine winners who were in the Top 10 with me were all amazing young women. I was honored to meet them and to see what they had accomplished. All of their stories were touching and inspiring. The mentors we met were all extremely successful and intelligent as well. I got to meet with people who simply offered insight on what it takes to accomplish big things in the real world and become even more influential throughout life.

I also especially enjoyed the hair and makeup experience! I got to meet and talk with a couple of well-known artists – it was a very relaxed and fun environment. I also was able to see a lot of New York City and what it has to offer. I learned a lot from the whole experience and it is something I will never be able to forget. It really changed my life and the outlook I had on it.

Throughout the experience all that I could think was WOW... I simply was raised right, worked hard in school and on the court, and gave back everything I could to my Native American people. I was being honored for being a good person and doing what is right. That means everything to me. It's not that I want the glory or attention, but it just makes me happy to realize that I am making a difference in others' lives and that is being recognized. At the end of the day, that's always been my goal; and when I found out I was selected for this prestigious honor I just couldn't believe it – simply because of where I had come from. When I was younger I never would've imagined that I would be in that position, and to see it all become a reality just humbles me and makes me want to do more for those who deserve it. It's not about the fame or the hype for me. It's about making other lives better because I'm in a position to do so.

I want to express the true happiness I felt on the last day of the seminar and awards. I remember not thinking about anything except for what was happening in the moment. All that I felt that day was joy. I was with nine other prestigious and sincere young women who were being honored for making a difference in the world. In addition to that, my parents and my sister were there with me, which made it that much sweeter. It's one experience that I will always hold dear to my heart. Being successful in sports is one thing, but to be honored for doing well in school and making a difference in society is so much more valuable to me. It really speaks volumes about the character of an individual and the way she was raised. I've always tried to be a good person and do what is right (even though it's not always easy), and to see all of my work and determination paying off was an amazing feeling of joy and happiness. It's surreal to think about where I started and where I am now.

THE MOVIE

Additionally, my family and I had another experience that would greatly affect our lives for a long time to come. We were approached by a film company to be featured in a documentary about our lives, with the focus being on Shoni and her attempt to earn a college basketball scholarship and succeed off the reservation. The backdrop would be our struggles that we face as Native Americans, the lack of opportunities for Native Americans on reservations, and our story of leaving reservation life.

At first my mom was very unsure of it and in the beginning she was actually against it. It was hard for us to move off the reservation, and she questioned whether or not she could trust the producers to accurately portray us. She was unsure about having a film crew follow our every move because one wrong impression may have allowed room for inaccurate assumptions and could have posed a threat to our futures. However, she and my dad had many meaningful and trusting conversations with producer Jon Hock, and he found a way to convince them, especially my mom, of how important this documentary could be. She then made the decision to trust her gut instinct and eventually said yes to the project.

I was actually sort of amazed at the fact that someone wanted to base a documentary on my sister and my family but because of the reasoning and intentions behind it, I was happy because I knew we were deserving of it. I was glad that they told my sister's story, and once we saw the movie I was glad they told the general story of our family as well because everything mentioned was significant in its own way to a variety of different audiences. The way I look at it is that it's not everyday someone comes into a family's household saying they want to make a documentary about them, but overall it was a really humbling opportunity and experience. To my family and me it wasn't about the fame or the glory. We feel that the more we can share our story about where we came from and how we got to where we are, the closer we will be to creating the lasting change that we want to see happen. Our hope is that Native Americans and anyone for that matter will follow their dreams, and live a happy, positive, healthy, and successful life.

The camera crews followed us around for about two years. Having cameras follow us around was a pretty cool experience, but toward the beginning I avoided them at all costs. Eventually though, the whole process of being filmed was actually quite casual and normal. Although it may have been slightly intimidating at first, I think everyone in my family got comfortable with it after a while. In addition, our whole family built very good relationships with Jon and each of the cameramen. They are some great people and they really did make the experience much easier and a lot more fun than I had originally imagined.

In April of 2011 my whole family and I were invited to attend the Tribeca Film Festival, which also meant the premiere showing of *Off The Rez*. This was quite an experience for all of us. We never really ever took family trips or vacations and most of us hadn't been anywhere but the west coast states such as Oregon, Washington, Idaho, and California. But this time we all took the trip and traveled to New York to share a very memorable experience together. It was really neat because we got to go sightseeing and do other fun things. We got to visit the Statue of Liberty, the Empire State Building, and Times Square. We also had the opportunity to attend a New York Yankees game, which was really fun. We even got to attend the television show *Live! With Regis and Kelly*, because Shoni's documentary was being mentioned during its airtime. To many people these types of things may seem normal and not anything special but to all of us it was an experience we would always remember and cherish. In addition to all of these things, we went to the Tribeca Film Festival and were a part of the premiere showing of *Off The Rez* which included a question and answer session with Shoni and my mom alongside a panel of Jon Hock, Kelly Ripa, and other significant people in the film industry. Also, prior to the event Shoni, my parents, and I were escorted to be a part of the red carpet event, which was really neat to be a part of. The overall experience was just very rare but also very special for myself and I'm sure for the rest of my family as well. I know it's something we will all remember and cherish for the rest of our lives. It was also apparent to me that this sort of marked the first "big" thing to happen to my family and which would eventually develop into many more great opportunities to have a positive impact on Native Americans across the country. I'm very thankful to Jon Hock, and everyone else who helped with the development and creation of the documentary because, through their compassion, I see hope and room for positive change in many people's lives.

MAKING A DIFFERENCE

As I've said so many times before, when I was younger I had no idea I would be in the position I am today. Through all of my life experiences, including growing up on the reservation, moving off the reservation, going to college, earning different awards and achieving the many humbling accomplishments that I have, I've been put in a position where other Native Americans view me as a role model. I view this as an honor, and because of it I have had the opportunity to travel around the country and speak to over forty different tribes, reservations, and communities.

The appearance opportunities started after the release of our family's documentary, *Off The Rez*, and it all began to really grow and expand after our 2013 run in the NCAA® tournament. In my opinion, out of all the things I've gained from going off to college and becoming successful, by far the most inspiring and influential thing for me is the fact that I have been blessed to be in a position where I can inspire and teach others to better their own lives. I try to set an example for others and tell them they can succeed by following their dreams, setting goals, and never settling for anything less than the best they deserve. As my family and me have traveled to all of these different places across the country, I have gained countless new experiences as well. I've gotten to see even more of the world than I already have from basketball. I've been able to share my story and my knowledge with others. I've seen some beautiful communities and cultures. And I've met some very great people through it all. I can't explain how significant these speaking events have been to my family and I. These experiences have been life changing and eye opening for me. As I mentioned, I have been able to witness some beautiful places and have been able to meet a lot of great people.

However, I have also seen the downside of Native American life as well. I've seen how the oppression of the past and present have and still are affecting my people. I've seen them struggling firsthand. And it hurts me to witness these types of things because I know we are a stronger, smarter, and much more beautiful people than the world has been able to see. Seeing the negativity has definitely made me want to share my story and knowledge with others even more to hopefully give them inspiration to go out and live a positive, happy, and healthy life. In addition to this, all the good that I've seen and all the good that I know about Native Americans gives me greater drive to do these types of things as well. To me, it's not about the fame. That's just how I was raised. It's not about money, status, prestige, or having control over anyone or anything. What I'm concerned with is the wellbeing of individuals, communities, and the greater good. I want to help others live a good life and live a life they've dreamed of for themselves. I know I can't change how people perceive Native Americans. I know I can't change how every Native American or individual perceives things or how they choose to approach life. I know I can't change the world overnight. But I know that if I can influence people one by one to make changes for the better, then eventually all those small sums will add up to something greater. Having the honor to be able to travel across the country to speak to so many Native Americans about my story and my family's story, and also to provide them with knowledge, inspiration, and hope that all these beautiful things in life are possible for them, has truly changed my life. As much as people may see me, my sister, and my family as inspiration, all the support we get from people across the country, especially the love and support we get from Native Americans, inspires me even more. It makes me want to do better and be better.

People have often asked me whether or not I feel pressure being in the position I am in as a high profile Native American. Of course there are times when feelings of stress or feelings of being overwhelmed come with the territory, but honestly ninety-nine percent of the time I don't feel any sense of pressure to be who I am. I was raised to be a good person, and I can thank my parents for that. The way they raised me has given me the ability to do all of these things with ease because most of the time it all comes so naturally to me. The values, skills, and priorities that have been instilled in me have given me this opportunity to be a role model to so many people. And the way I see it is that I was put in this position for a reason. I feel like it is all much bigger than myself, and I know that what I'm doing is the right thing. I know that it will all pay off in the end by positively impacting Native Americans and hopefully many others.

Most important, I want to share how much the speaking events I've participated in have positively influenced my life. Being able to see all the things and places that I have, all the beautiful people I've met along the way, and all of the experiences and new things I've learned have honestly made me into a better person. They've made me grow and accept the position I am in even more than I already had. They've helped me become even more appreciative of where I came from. They've made me proud of my culture and heritage. And most important, they have inspired me to want to continue to be the best possible person I can be and to make a difference for myself, my family, and every other Native American out there who has a goal or dream they wish to achieve and accomplish. I will continue to work to make a difference in others' lives, and pray that God guides me in the right direction to put things into perspective and create a world of opportunity, happiness, and success for as many other people as I possibly can.

PART 1: MY STORY

WHITE HOUSE

Generation Indigenous (GEN-I), a new partnership between the White House and the Center of Native American Youth (CNAY), was recently created and announced in the Fall of 2014 by President Barack Obama. It is the very first ever to be created for Native Americans in the United States. Those who are involved range from significant government officials, philanthropists and sponsors, to native youth and tribal leaders from various tribes and reservations. All of the efforts are dedicated towards positive change in a variety of fields such as education and health for Native Americans across the country.

The Generations Indigenous Convening and Initiative took place on April 8th 2015 at the White House in Washington, DC. I was extremely honored to be invited and to be involved in the event. It was honestly one of the very best experiences of my life. The whole time I was there all I could think to myself was, "wow, this is exactly where I'm supposed to be." Ever since I was a young girl I've been concerned with the issues that revolve around Native Americans and our communities. I've always hoped and wished to be able to help change these negatives to positives for my people and being invited to the GEN-I Initiative by multiple parties involved in the event I am extremely humbled and excited. I really feel like I am finally in a position to help make a significant difference in other people's lives. I can't explain how honored, relieved, and ready I am to take action toward creating a better future for all Native Americans across the country.

My trip to Washington, DC was so amazing in all aspects. The first thing I got to do in the morning was meet the First Lady, Michelle Obama. It was very short and brief but I was lucky enough to speak to her for a few seconds and get my picture taken with her. After that she gave the opening speech of the event and I was so blown away by it. Everything she mentioned and every issue she touched on was exactly all of things I've been wanting to share with the rest of the world. It was so similar to many things I discuss in this book that I really couldn't believe it. I am relieved and excited that the issues Native Americans have been faced with for so long are finally being recognized by the government and other people with power in our society. It gives me hope that change is coming.

After the First Lady gave her speech the event went into panels and round table discussions which were based around some of the most prevalant issues going on in Native American communities. Everyone involved that day was solely focused on what we as individuals and as a whole can do to help create more opportunities and better futures for Native Americans and the future generations. At the end of the event I had the honor to speak for a few minutes to the whole group and also announce the GEN-I Initiative video.

The way I see it is that this day was one of the most important days of my life. And it had nothing to do with the status or prestige that may have been involved. I was sincerely just so happy and so relieved that these issues have reached and been recognized by the President, the First Lady, and the White House. As I mentioned before I really felt like I was in the exact place I was meant to be. I had the chance to meet and network with so many different and great people who all had the same goals and hopes as myself. I can't express how genuinely happy and thankful I was that day to be apart of something so special.

As soon as my college career ended I really thought I would have a little bit of time to just calm down, relax, and catch my breath. But that wasn't the case at all. My life became busier than ever instantly as my basketball season came to an end. I finished up writing my book, I was invited to the White House, I was still finishing classes for my master's degree, and I became an Ambassador for Nike N7 which is a branch of Nike that is dedicated towards bettering the lives of Native Americans especially in the manner of physical fitness. To be honest the list doesn't stop there, but I really believe everything happens for a reason and although I may be busy I am beyond thankful to be in the position I am and I am looking forward to what the future has to bring for myself and for Native Americans across the country.

PART 2:

———————————————

MY LESSONS

In Part I of this book, I told about my story of overcoming the odds and succeeding outside of the reservation. I shared my story and some of my accomplishments in order to show you that these types of things can be done regardless of where you come from. In the following pages of Part II, I wanted to share how I was able to succeed and also some of the lessons I was taught early on, as well as lessons I learned through my own experiences. I've always appreciated inspirational quotes because they simplify the often overwhelming and complicated aspects of life. I've chosen a few of my favorite ones to help convey some words of wisdom based upon my own experiences.

I feel as though if people can find a way to take a step back and clearly think about this kind of stuff, then they can begin to realize how simple life really can be. I'm not perfect and I never will be, but I have learned from my mistakes and my experiences. I feel like a lot of people aren't always capable of doing this because they can't step back and reflect clearly without their emotions or assumptions getting in the way. I'm not asking anyone to be perfect or to be like me. All I'm asking is that you try to do the right thing for yourself, for those you love and care about, and for the greater good. I'm asking that you try to implement these things into your life and then watch to see if change happens, or to see if there's progress being made. If the answer is no then I am wrong and you can call me crazy. But if the answer is yes then go out and live your life to the fullest and share with as many others the lessons you've learned along the way. Tell them what it took for you to get to where you are. Tell them what it takes to fully and truly catch a dream.

I know that I don't even come close to covering all of the issues that life entails, but I chose to include some of the ones that are most significant to me in hopes that my insight will help others in their own lives to begin to strive for happiness, good health, and success.

PART 2: MY LESSONS

DREAMS~GOALS~PASSIONS

The best way to predict your future is to create it.

Everything starts with having a passion for something. Everyone has something they are passionate about and love doing or participating in. Whatever that may be, embrace it and keep it a priority in your life. Even if you think you aren't very good at it or even if you don't think it's possible to do or make anything out of it, keep it a priority and keep working for it. You will be amazed at how good you can get at something if you work at it constantly and repeatedly. Also, I've learned that it's the ones who think outside the box and go out on limbs that end up making something out of nothing. Some of the most successful ideas, companies, and businesses have come from one single person who simply had a dream and chose to pursue it.

My favorite example to share about dreams and passions is my sister Shoni's passion for basketball. When Shoni was a little girl, she always talked about how she just wanted to play basketball for a living. She idolized the greatest players of all time: the big-time players like Michael Jordan, Cynthia Cooper, LeBron James, and Candace Parker. She would always try to imitate their moves and implement their skills into her own game. This started at age 4, and it continued up until her senior year of college when she ended up being the 8th overall pick of the first round of the 2014 WNBA draft. She also was the 2014 WNBA All-Star Game MVP. Both during the draft and during that All Star game, all I could think was, "Wow - my sister made her dream a reality!" But let me tell you this, it was by no means an easy thing to accomplish. We grew up on a tiny Native American Indian reservation in eastern Oregon with no type of exposure to the basketball "real world" with scouts and coaches. We had to endure different forms of prejudice and discrimination throughout the years, and my family lacked money.

But with the help of my parents, through hard work and dedication, and of course with the right moves, time, and opportunity, everything worked out for her. Her dream to be a professional basketball player since she was a little girl became a reality at the age of twenty-two. I can't explain how happy and how proud I was of her for making it that far. But even more important, I want others to realize that if Shoni and I can work to make a dream a reality, then so can they. We didn't have a red carpet laid out for us, and we didn't grow up with a silver spoon in our mouths. Of course, we had our parents who did everything they could to set us up to be successful, but we still had to work hard and we had to remain determined not to allow outside distractions or obstacles to get in our way.

The process of making your dream a reality is as simple as you want to make it. There are certain things you must do, but the good thing is the most important choices are completely within your control. You get to make the decision of what you want to do. You control your effort and your attitude. You decide if every second of hard work and focus toward your goal is worth it or not. There will be distractions and ups and downs along the way, but you can't allow yourself to become affected by these things. You must remain focused on your goal and remain determined to reach it. Most important, you have to start somewhere. If you have a dream or goal, achieving it starts with the decision to try then from there you simplify it and move forward one step at a time.

To make it easier and less overwhelming or stressful, set a goal for yourself. Set goals for yourself every day, every week, and every month. Have a plan laid out for yourself and be disciplined enough to stick to it. Over the years I've learned that being self-disciplined is one huge key to success. Being a student athlete I realized there was a lot going on in my life: practice, classes, social life, homework, sport events, etc. This is just my example but generally speaking it's easy to get distracted by things like wanting to hang out with your friends instead of getting in the gym or wanting to sleep instead of doing your homework. It's normal, and those types of distractions appear to everyone. Distractions are always going to be there, and you will always have the decision to make of whether or not you take the easy route and get distracted, or if you are going to do what gets you one step closer to reaching your goal and catching your dreams. But like I said, if you wish to get somewhere or do something with your life, you have to start somewhere. The hardest step is the first one. Once you're able to take it, the rest is about keeping yourself focused and on track.

Eventually, one day at a time, one step at a time, you will slowly begin to see your dreams becoming a reality -- and let me tell you, it is a beautiful thing and an amazing feeling. I still get that feeling today. Sometimes I really can't believe where I came from and how far I've come. It is all such a blessing. And I promise you, you can do it. And you will be so proud of yourself if you just buckle down and do what's best for you and your life. I've probably said this a million times already but I'll say it again: it's not going to be easy. It may be hard and it may take a lot of sacrifice, discipline, focus, and determination. But I promise you it will be worth it. If you love what you are doing and you truly want to achieve something meaningful, all of your hard work and effort will pay off and you will be satisfied. So if you ever get distracted or begin to doubt yourself, just remember that the pain of discipline and hard work are far less than the pain of regret. If you have a dream in your heart follow it, believe that you can do it, and pray about it. The way I see it is that prayer is necessary and a wonderful thing, and the combination of prayer and hard work will set you up for success. This all goes back to being disciplined enough and wise enough to know that great things take balance. A mixture of the right tools will get you to where you desire to be.

Another thing I would like to touch on is the fact that oftentimes people allow age, race, geographic location, or other factors to become reasons or excuses as to why they don't think their goals or dreams are possible to reach. I feel sad when I see this type of thing – and I see it a lot. I am telling you that you can overcome any obstacle if you put your mind to it. Age is nothing but a number, and if you have goals for yourself or a dream to accomplish don't let your age stop you – or anything for that matter. From going back to school to traveling the country, whatever your goal may be, find a way to do it. Take the chance, because taking a risk is so much more fulfilling than being stagnant, content, and stuck with a life less than you imagined for yourself. Things like discrimination and prejudice will always be underlying issues in our society, but those things will never influence you if you do everything the right way for yourself. Don't allow the glass ceiling and barriers to affect your success. Do the little things right, focus on what really matters, ignore ignorant individuals, control what you can control and focus on your goal. Through my experiences I've learned these types of issues will take care of themselves if you just make yourself realize that you have no control over them.

Many people, especially Native Americans, live in rural places without the most modern accommodations. Don't let things like this become excuses for you to settle. Living in a rural place cannot be the reason you don't make something of yourself. I'm not saying everyone is going to be able to pack up and leave their home to move somewhere with more exposure and opportunity like my family did, but one way or another you need to allow yourself that opportunity. Using a basketball example, perhaps you're a Native American living on a reservation and you have a goal to pursue basketball at a higher level like Shoni and me. Make a plan for your situation and go for it. Whether it means playing on a team that gets that exposure, using technology to get your name out to coaches and scouting services, or simply expanding your network, there are endless things you can do that will help create more opportunity for yourself. But as I've said over and over, it will be hard, because nothing worth having comes easy. Find a way to make things possible for yourself. Don't take short cuts. Take the necessary steps and do what is right and not what is easy. Nothing will ever be perfect, but in the end it will all be worth it and you will be so much happier living the life you dreamed of rather than settling for anything less than that.

WORK ETHIC

*The difference between who you are and who you want to be
is the amount of work you put in.*

Very few people have ever achieved anything meaningful in life without working hard and having a strong work ethic. Hard work, resiliency, and strength are all extremely important contributors to solid work ethics. I had to work extremely hard to get to where I am in my life. There may always be someone else who is bigger, faster, stronger, and smarter than you but here's a quote to help put things into perspective: "Hard work beats talent when talent fails to work hard." My work ethic has helped me overcome my drawbacks and achieve a basketball scholarship while playing at the highest Division I college level. If I didn't work hard, I would never have earned a college scholarship or played at a top-notch basketball program such as the University of Louisville. My hard work also helped me graduate from college in three years and enabled me to pursue a Masters degree in Sports Administration. I really believe my parents instilled a strong work ethic in me and I take pride in trying to work harder than anyone else not because I am in any competition with them but simply because I know my abilities and I know what I am trying to achieve. This mindset and work ethic allowed me to accomplish great things in the classroom as well. In addition to graduating in three years, I was able to earn the Final Four Elite 89 award for academic excellence. Through my experiences I've realized that it isn't about who is the smartest or most gifted at any particular thing, rather life is about who works the hardest at achieving their goals. Hard work is crucial if you wish to do significant things in your life. It will directly contribute to reaching your goals and achieving your dreams. I would not have been able to attend college, play college basketball, or earn a degree without having a good work ethic. I would not have been able to write this book about my life experiences and what I've learned from them without lots of hard work along the way.

Another very measurable example of my hard work paying off is in my three-point shooting. During my freshman season at UofL, I lost a lot of confidence in my ability to shoot and I only shot about 16% from the three-point line. However, I was determined to regain my confidence despite what my role was "supposed to be." I worked hard every season and offseason, and especially focused on improving my shooting during the summer before my senior year. The hard work ended up paying off, and at one point towards the middle of the season I was shooting about 40% from the three-point line. This is also an example of how crucial confidence is when it comes to meaningful accomplishments.

Beyond those examples, really anything I've ever done well in I've worked extremely hard for. I think a strong work ethic will contribute to success in any goal you are trying to achieve. It doesn't have to be sports at all. Find what you are passionate about, apply hard work and you will see results. And hard work is something you can control. No one else can work hard for you or make the decision for you to work hard for yourself.

You have to work for what you want as nothing in life is going to be handed to you. I always tell people that getting an education wasn't necessarily the easiest thing for me to do. I understand I am smart, but I still had to work extremely hard to get good grades and to do well in school.

Lastly I just want to say that you can't let the little stuff get in your way of working hard and attempting to reach your goals. Everyone will have daily struggles and everyone can find excuses during the course of the day to not work hard but you can't allow these types of things to keep you from achieving all that you are capable of.

PART 2: MY LESSONS

CONFIDENCE

Too many days are wasted comparing ourselves to others and wishing to be something we aren't. Everybody has their own strengths and weaknesses and it is only when you accept everything you are - and aren't - that you will truly succeed.

I can't stress how important confidence is to one's happiness and success. In my opinion everyone has both strengths and weaknesses. That's just how we are as humans and like I've said many times before we can only control certain things in our lives, and those are the things we should all focus on. I feel like too many people waste time comparing their lives and situations to others, and it's true that comparison is the thief of joy. If we waste time comparing ourselves to others, we take away from the focus of our own lives. Rather than hoping, wishing and thinking about things we don't have or the things we wish we could have, why not think about the things we do have and the things we can control? Having confidence is crucial if you wish to do great things with your life. There are going to be times in your life when people will doubt you and your ability, but if you have confidence within yourself that will solve over half of the battle you are facing.

It is also important to learn to accept our weaknesses and use our strengths to our advantage. There is a reason why everyone has different gifts, talents, characteristics, etc., but as individuals we have to appreciate the gifts we've been blessed with and not stress about the ones we don't possess. Of course there is always room for improvement in any area of life, but that's a whole other piece to the process of building strong self-confidence. You have to practice and prepare yourself prior to the challenges you're going to be faced with. It's okay not to be the best at everything, but you should never settle for less than your personal best. You can't sit around wishing and praying that you will get someone else's talents, skills, looks, or their life. That's simply not going to happen. We were all made different for a reason and we need to embrace that.

Be proud of yourself. Love yourself. And believe in yourself. You have to believe that you have the ability to do whatever you wish to do in life. You can't listen to the negativity of other people. Learn to ignore the negative and ignorant noise in your life and focus on the positive. Focus on what you are good at. Focus on what you want to be good at and work your butt off to get to the point where you can achieve your goal. Whether it's getting good grades, doing well in sports, or simply just trying to get into better shape, you have to have the confidence to do all of that yourself. Take everything one step at a time. It's not always going to be easy, but if you believe in yourself and have the confidence in yourself to achieve that goal then eventually you will get there. There have been many times in my life I've questioned my own ability. But I've always found a way to get past that doubt. That's what I want for everyone. I want people to be content with themselves and confident enough in themselves to make a commitment to achieving their goals. And I know it's so much easier said than done. I know it's easy to be insecure. I know it's easy to want what others have. But what I tell myself is that I am the way I am for a reason. I was blessed with my own certain qualities just like everyone else. We were meant to be unique.

Another thing I tell myself is I shouldn't always do what is easy. Rather than wanting something else, I tell myself to accept myself for who I am, embrace that and make the most of it. For example, on the basketball court I have never been the biggest, strongest, or the most skilled. But I do know what my strengths are when it comes to basketball. I know that I may be small, but I see it as an advantage and that's partially why I've been able to be successful on the court. I realized and focused on my strengths, and used them to my own advantage rather than wishing and hoping that I could be taller than what I am. There is a quote that says "It's not who you are that holds you back, it's what you think you are not." That is so true, and all I can say is that you have to love yourself and embrace the gifts you have been blessed with. I'm not saying to settle, and I'm not saying to give up on your dreams just because you're not tall enough or not smart enough or whatever it might be. I'm saying embrace yourself. Be proud of who you are and what you have. And if there is anything worth having you can go out and work for it. I really can't express how important confidence is to the direction in which your life goes. It plays a huge role in determining how happy you can be and how successful you can become. If you want to make something of yourself and live a life you've imagined you have to believe in yourself first. You have to ignore the negativity and you have to work for what you want. Make it all possible. But, most important, you have to accept yourself. There is nothing wrong with who you are, but only you can truly convince yourself of that. No one is perfect. Learn to accept your weaknesses and embrace your strengths. Relish those strengths and use them to your advantage. With the right mixture of hard work and preparation, someday all of the love and confidence in yourself will pay off, and someday you will achieve that goal you've always had.

PART 2: MY LESSONS

OVERCOMING ADVERSITY

It is your reaction to adversity, not the adversity itself
that determines how your life's story will develop.

Dealing with adversity is one of the ultimate challenges in life. Everyone faces adversity at some point in their lives, and most people deal with it off and on constantly day in and day out. It's normal and it happens to everyone. So next time you are feeling stressed, upset, helpless, or overwhelmed, make yourself relax. It's okay to have moments of heartache or hurt. Everybody, and I mean every single human being on this planet, has breakdowns. But after you have your moment you need to let it go and find a way to move past it. I'm not saying you have to forget or ignore whatever happened. What I'm saying is don't allow it to consume you and don't allow it to take a longer toll on you than it should. There will be infinite moments of disappointment, hurt feelings, prejudice, discrimination, and other forms of adversity thrown at you, but what I've learned over the years from my experiences and from my parents is that bad things are going to happen and things you don't agree with are going to happen. These types of things are meant to challenge you. And it is how you react that really defines who you are. The way I see it is anybody can do well when things are going their way or if they have some type of advantage, but where the true strength lies is in those who keep fighting; the ones who never give up.

We can't allow the unfortunate and negative things in life to hold us back or keep us from living a good life. So whatever adversity may be present in your life, whether it's related to family, a relationship, school, bad habits, work, or you just overthinking, whatever it may be let it go and learn from it. I could give countless examples of overcoming adversity but the one that always comes to mind is my parents. My parents have been through SO much I still have a hard time grasping it all and understanding how the heck they did and still do all that they've done for themselves, their family, their friends, and so many others. I admire them so much. They have displayed so much strength and perseverance just through their actions that I don't need to know anything else to have respect for them. A white man being with a Native American woman in the late 80's and early 90's wasn't exactly something people admired. Even some of my dad's own family wouldn't accept my parents being together. Some of the things my parents had to deal with don't even seem real to me, but the fact that they now have 8 kids and see their kids doing well makes me feel much better. In knowing that their hard work and perseverance and sacrifices paid off makes me feel that all of the adversity they went through was all meant to happen, and all the good that came back to them was just their karma coming back around.

So as I've said before, regardless of whatever might be going wrong in your life, and whatever type of adversity you may be going through, just remember that everything happens for a reason. Each of these moments of adversity are a challenge for you to grow as an individual. Either you can take control of your situation and face the challenge head-on, or it will find a way to control you and take over your life. Everyone goes through ups and downs in life and everyone is going to handle situations of adversity differently. But people need to find a way to just take a step back and realize their reaction is so much more significant than the adversity they are dealing with. And trust me, I know all of this sounds so much easier said than done, but it is possible to handle things this way, and I can say that because I've experienced it. I've been told over and over that I'm too small to be successful in basketball and I've dealt with coaches not giving me playing time because they thought I wasn't good enough, but somehow

I became a significant part of one of the best Division I teams in the country. I've dealt with ignorant individuals displaying acts of racism, prejudice and discrimination against my family and me. I've also dealt with being betrayed by some of the people I thought I was closest to, but I never let any of this define me as an individual. Because of how I was raised and the experiences I've had, I've been able to learn that through adversity is where true strength is built. And this all goes back to having self-confidence and a purpose in your life. If you believe in yourself and know what you want to attain in life, then you can teach yourself to handle adversity with class. You can teach yourself how to control your thoughts, your feelings, and your reaction to anything you may be faced with. But it all starts with you. You have to commit to making yourself think a certain way and you have to teach yourself how to be prepared for the times in your life that will challenge you.

The last thing I want to touch on in this part is letting go of the past. I know so many people -- family, friends, strangers -- who cannot escape their past. They continuously allow their past to haunt them and affect their present and their future – and I hate it. I can't stand to see people allow their past to take over their lives and have such a huge impact on the decisions they make or the feelings they feel. I understand that it's natural for humans to become overwhelmed with the hurt they've felt or the unfairness they've been faced with. I truly do sympathize with people who have been mistreated and hurt, and I honestly believe everyone deserves to have a shoulder to cry and lean on. They deserve to have their moments where they break down and vent, and feel sorry for themselves, because I know how hard it can be at times. I've seen the ugly sides of life and that's exactly why I'm telling people that they need to find a way to let the negativity of their past go and move forward. The past will always be the past and there is absolutely nothing you or anybody else can do about it. It's up to you not to allow these negative things to repeat themselves. If something bad happens to you or your life you can have your moment of feeling down, but after that you need to get back up, dust yourself off, and move on with your life.

Every thought you think and every decision you make is shaping your future, and you owe it to yourself to let it go. You owe it to yourself to let go of all that pain and heartache: holding onto it won't get you to where you want to be. I know it hurts and I know how hard it can be to move on from something that once affected you so significantly, but if you don't then you will continuously allow something you have no control over to consume you and your life. Like I said before, bad things happen to everyone and everyone is faced with the ups and downs of life; that's just how it is. Somebody may deal with a different form of adversity than you do, but that doesn't mean it's any easier. Don't compare your hurt to the hurt of others. There is a reason we go through the things we do. And there comes a point where you either choose to let it go, learn from it and grow, or else you will forever be stuck living a life of stress and unhappiness. I know you can't control what happens to you, and I know it's not easy to accept that or deal with. But, luckily for us, we can control how we react. Even better for us, we get to choose in which direction our life goes next. Be strong. And be perseverant.

After all, every storm runs out of rain.

PART 2: MY LESSONS

POSITIVITY

*The only difference between a good day
and a bad day is your attitude.*

If there is one thing I've learned over the last few years that I would really like to share with other people, it would be that your attitude and perspective are everything. I used to be an individual who let the little things get to me, and I would let the things I have no control over bother me and overwhelmingly stress me out. There are a million different examples I could give, but I believe most people know exactly what I'm talking about and most people can probably relate to it. There are always going to be things that have the potential to upset you or make your life stressful. But, if we can learn to control our thoughts and train our minds to focus on the positive, then we will begin to see change in our lives. I know how easy it is to let things get to you. As humans we want things to be ideal and match the ideas we have in our head. We want, hope, and expect things to go a certain way in our lives. But I think most people realize that this isn't always the case. There are going to be times in our lives when life doesn't go how we want it to. There are going to be situations that you don't like, and there are going to be things you don't agree with. The way I see it is that there are two ways to handle these challenges we're faced with: you can either allow them to ruin things for you, or you simply learn from them and grow. Pretty much up until my sophomore year in college I would allow the little things to ruin my days, but as I've begun to mature I've realized that I have to find the positive in everything. There is always something positive that comes from every situation, whether the situation itself is good or bad.

I know it's natural as humans to have a roller coaster of thoughts, feelings, and emotions. Everybody goes through highs and lows in their lives, and that's just how it is. But, in my opinion, it's how we handle the lows that makes the biggest difference. Rather than allowing the negativity to get to you, rather than overthinking or wishing you could've done something different or handled a situation differently, try to accept the fact that whatever does happen happens for a reason. In addition, try to focus on the positive and focus on what you can learn from the hard times in your life. I've already said this many times, but it's worth repeating: Don't just do what's easy; don't just take the easy route. Challenge yourself to be a strong individual. If you can learn to control your thoughts and how you view things, you give yourself the chance to live a happier life. Your thoughts are where it all starts. If you can keep your thoughts positive, regardless of whatever may happen those thoughts will become habitual and they will carry over into your words and your actions. If you take a step back to really think about this it all plays into the decisions you make, and essentially it all affects the process and outcome of your life. I'm talking about the big picture here. Every thought you think, every decision you make in every second and every minute of every day… all of these slowly begin to add up and make up the outcome of your life.

I'm not saying everyone will always be able to be optimistic and chipper about things in life. What I'm saying is you have control of how much negativity impacts your life. You don't always have control over what happens to you, but you do have the power to control the direction in which your life goes. You have to approach it one step at a time. I really just want to tell people not to take life too seriously all of the time. Of course you want to be ambitious and hard-working, but at the end of the day life is about balance and being happy with yourself and the life you live. You can't do that unless you have a positive approach to it all. Therefore, learn to let go of what holds you back. Let go of what you can't control. Ignore negativity or learn from it. Life isn't always going to be good and easy; therefore be open to challenges and when life throws obstacles at you, find a way to overcome them. Elevate yourself and your life by being positive and making the best of every situation. We have to appreciate our lives and what we have. You also need to be thankful for where you are in life, and if you're not happy with your situation then change it. I keep preaching about staying positive and seeing the good in everything but if you wish to better your life you have to take the initiative for yourself. Once you realize the power is within your own reach nothing and no one can make you act, think, or feel any certain way. As I've said many times before it starts with what you allow yourself to think and at the end of the day all it's really about is being able to take a step back and realize that the complexity of life can be made simple when you put things into perspective and make yourself focus on the right stuff.

PART 2: MY LESSONS

KEEP MOVING FORWARD

If you can't fly, then run, if you can't run then walk,
if you can't walk then crawl. But whatever you do,
you have to keep moving forward.

Potential is a scary thing. And as humans I think we tend to underestimate ourselves based on inaccurate and stereotypical measurements of ability. In other words, we become intimidated about certain things and then begin to question whether or not we have the ability to overcome obstacles or whether or not we have the potential to improve a skill or succeed at something that challenges us. One thing that's important to understand and accept is that everyone is different and everyone has different talents, intentions, and goals in life. But there is also one thing everyone has in common: the fact that there is always more room to grow and improve in whatever it is we are doing with our lives.

People come from all sorts of backgrounds and situations. However, the true fact of the matter lies not necessarily in where you come from, but more so in how you can continue to grow and move forward. Everybody wants to accomplish or attain something in life. What that is for one person may very well be different for the next. But one thing we've all probably learned along the way is that reaching that goal isn't exactly easy. Life will throw things at you and it may challenge you emotionally, physically, mentally, socially, financially, or whatever it may be. There will be times in your life when you question whether or not you can handle these obstacles you've been faced with. There is an infinite amount of reasons why someone can be stressed out or feel like giving up, but in those moments of doubt you have to force yourself to stay grounded. Remember your purpose and why you started the journey toward your goal in the first place. You have to understand that it's normal to face obstacles and that it's normal to have moments of doubt or confusion. But more important, you need to understand that what has happened up to that point has all happened for a reason, and it's up to you to decide which direction your life will go next. You can either allow the doubt to build up and chase you away from pursuing your goals, or you can decide that you were meant for this and that you really do have the power to overcome whatever you are being faced with. The biggest thing is that whatever life throws at you, you can't let it scare you away from following your dreams. Everyone has the idea in their head of what kind of life they want to live, and in any moment of doubt just stay focused on that idea. Any time I begin to feel stressed out or overwhelmed I just tell myself to think about how badly I want to live a happy and successful life. Rather than letting the stress take over, I make myself remember why I started working toward my goal in the first place and why I want to achieve it. So make yourself think about what you need to do to make your dreams a reality, and let that fuel you to work harder toward reaching your goals. Like I said before, people may be in a different situation than you, they may have it much easier than you, but you can't let that stop you.

I grew up on a tiny reservation in eastern Oregon. Most people have no idea where it is or know that it even exists. But, I never stopped trying to be the best that I could be especially when it came to school, sports, and just being a good person. Eventually, my hard work started to pay off and it was recognized. And I never allowed myself to settle even after I got my scholarship to attend the University of Louisville. There were so many times I could've given up or just been content with where I was in terms of basketball skill and even as a person in general, but I never stopped trying to better myself. I kept moving forward and challenging myself to be a better individual in every possible way. I've never been perfect and I never will be, but the only reason I've been able to accomplish so many things in my life is because I've never allowed myself to settle. And that's what I want people to understand: that there is always room to improve yourself and your situation. There is always hope to reach your goals so long as you work hard and stay focused on what you are trying to accomplish.

I know life isn't easy. I know it isn't always fair, and I know that everyone is faced with different struggles day in and day out. But, at the end of the day, we can't allow these types of things to keep us from becoming all that we were meant to be. You have a goal and you have a purpose in this life. You know what you want and you know what you need to get there. This is me telling you that you can and that you should. Don't let doubt, criticism or anything else keep you from reaching your goals. And always, always stay looking up. Life isn't as bad as we may think it is at times, and as I've said so many times before, it really is up to us as individuals to make the decision to pursue the life we wish to live.

Finally, here is a quote to help you get started.

"Tomorrow is too late. Yesterday is over.
Now, is exactly the right moment to start."

Don't be afraid. Just get started and whatever you do keep moving forward.

PART 2: MY LESSONS

CHOICES

*The time will pass anyway. You can either spend it
creating the life you want, or spend it living the life you don't want,
but the choice is ultimately yours.*

You may not realize it now but every single thought you think is creating your future and every single thing you do will have an impact on the outcome of your life. And every choice you make will affect you. There will be things and people that will impact your life both positively and negatively, but you can't allow these to control you or the choices you make. Of course I think it's important to take things into consideration and to be open to new things, but at the end of the day it's all up to you. It's up to you to get up in the morning and to get a goodnight's sleep. It's up to you whether you eat healthy or unhealthy. It's up to you whether you take care of yourself. It's up to you what thoughts you think. It's up to you what you choose to do. It's up to you what you say, and how you handle things. It's up to you whether you wake up and go to school every day. It's up to you if you practice. It's up to you if you do your homework. It's up to you if you choose to have fun or take care of business. It's up to you what kind of fun you choose to have. It's up to you what friends you have and who you let influence you. It's up to you if you show up on time. It's up to you what you choose to value. It's up to you how you respond to situations. It's literally all up to you. And whether you believe it or whether you realize it, every little thing makes a difference. It all matters. I'm not asking or telling people to live a perfect life, there is no such thing. What I'm suggesting is to learn to control your thoughts. Realize that you have control of the direction in which your life goes. You have the power to live a life you want, rather than living a life of negativity that is full of stress, unhappiness, inequality, or any other negative thing.

Anything can happen. But, generally speaking, everyone wants to live a good and desirable life. Remember though, it's not about how badly you want it. It's about how hard you are willing to work for it. Anyone can say they want something or want to achieve something in life, but what separates individuals is how hard we work and how much time and effort we put into the goal we are trying to reach. Therefore "ask yourself if what you are doing today is getting you closer to where you want to be tomorrow."

Life may not be fair, and things aren't equal in this society. However, there are some things that are completely true. Everyone gets the same twenty-four hours in a day, and everyone gets the same seven days a week. What you choose to do with that time is what makes the difference. It may sound cliché, but you can't deny something that is as concrete as that statement. Therefore, place your focus on what matters and use your time wisely so that you can create a life you desire to live.

Additionally, people need to choose to learn to let go of the past. I've mentioned this before. I know what Native Americans have been through. I also know what has happened to all other racial and ethnic groups of people throughout history. There's not any group who hasn't had to deal with some type of unfair and harsh treatment. Bad things happen to everyone. There are different levels of hurt, and everyone's situations and lives are different. There is no sense to continuously comparing our lives with others when that's just the way things are. We can't change the past. We can't continue to dwell on things that we have no control over. Choose to let the past go. Choose to focus on the future. Build and create the future you want rather than allowing all of the pain and sorrow of your past or present to hold you back. Make the most of what's going to happen instead of worrying about what you can't change. History can't be erased, but the future has yet to be written.

Without a doubt change is necessary sometimes. You have to be willing to make a change if you want to see change. "Progress is impossible without change, and those who cannot change their minds cannot change anything."

If you think your life is hard, please remember that God gives His hardest battles to His strongest soldiers. Don't let the negativity in the world discourage you from becoming what you were meant to be or what you want to be. Give it all you've got. Be willing to work for it. There's a process and a path to success. There are necessary tools to experience happiness and live happily. You have to be strong if you want it to persist. I believe that "God would not have put a dream in your heart if He hadn't already given you everything you need to fulfill it."

Additionally, knowing what you deserve is pointless if you aren't disciplined enough and willing to work for it. Settling for less than you are capable of won't get you what you hope to achieve. People often want things to become easier rather than choosing to put in the work and finding the strength to fight through hard times. This is the reason why people rarely get what they want. What are you willing to work for and earn? How much time and effort are you willing to put forth in order to find the happiness and success you want and deserve? Your commitment towards building a foundation and creating the life you want to live is everything. Learn what it takes to get there. Do what it takes to live a life you desire. It's okay to be scared, nervous, or uncertain. Whatever happens was meant to happen. Therefore, remember your goals, remember your purpose and your strength. If you truly want something, persistence and resilience are necessary. Don't force it but if you want something and it was meant for you it will find a way to work out. You just have to have the faith and wisdom to know what is meant for you and what is not.

Don't allow the struggles of everyday life to take over your mind. Every moment and every day is a new one. Choose to change your mind. Choose to alter your attitude, your behavior and your life choices to be compatible with how you want to live and what you want to achieve, accomplish, and attain in life. Keep your mind positive. Stay grounded in your beliefs. Stay driven by whatever your passion may be. Choose to stay positive through adversity because ups and downs are just a part of life. There is a saying that life is 10% of what happens to you and 90% of how you handle it. It's true. Only you have true and ultimate control over certain things. Simply put: "Stress is a choice. Joy is a choice. Therefore, make sure you choose wisely."

PART 2: MY LESSONS

EDUCATION

The true purpose of education is to make minds, not careers.
-William Deresiewicz

In my opinion, there is a variety of definitions and understandings when people hear the word "education." And I feel like, over time, the meaning of education has changed. In today's society, ninety-nine percent of the time a person's education is what determines the quality of job they will get. This directly plays a large role in the outcome of their life in every aspect including the house they live in, the car they drive, etc. Essentially, this all plays into the happiness and success of a person's life. Earning an education is one of the most significant accomplishments a person can have in life. While I think that education is extremely important, I think our society has lost its way on what it means to be truly educated. For example, the way the school systems are set up, it seems that it's not what you learn but rather what you can memorize that's important. Or in other words, schools aren't worried about what students actually learn because they are more concerned with what grades they earn; this attitude shows how the essence of education is missing in our school systems. As I said, education is extremely important to me and I'm not denying the fact that people should value their education. It's just that I believe as a whole, society should be more concerned with the essence of education and not the status it gives people.

On another note, education is extremely important for two reasons. One, you need an education to live the life you want or a good life, which I'm sure we can all picture what that looks like. And secondly, education is simply what fuels our society and our economy. It's important to learn and gain knowledge about different things because it will help us live overall better lives. Going back to the first point of why education is important: You're not going to change society overnight therefore we need to accept it for what it is right now and make the most of it. In this society without an education you're not going to be able to live a life you want if you don't do well in school. You need an education to do well in this society. You don't get hired for a job unless you have an education. You need money to buy a house, you need money to buy a car, you need money to feed your family, etc. but you need a job to be able to earn that money. And it all starts with getting a solid education. And all of that starts when you're young. Of course elementary and middle school years may not be as significant but that's when you begin to build your foundation. Then once you get to high school is when you really need to make school a priority and do well. I know it's easy to blow off homework and I know having fun or relaxing is much more desirable, but your high school days are where it truly starts. By getting good grades in high school you make room for so many opportunities and possibilities for yourself. I've always valued grades, but in high school I truly did do everything I could to get the best grades possible. And by doing that I was able to receive multiple scholarship offers. Think about it: I came from a family of 8 children. My parents weren't wealthy at all, nor were my grandmas. There was no possibility for them to pay for college tuition. And I knew that by getting good grades I would make college an option for myself. Obviously I ended up getting a basketball scholarship but not everyone is going to have an athletic scholarship opportunity. And there is absolutely nothing wrong with that because there are other scholarships you can get simply by getting good grades. I really can't stress how important good grades are, and the sooner you realize that, the better position you will be in to make your dream life a reality. Education can complement and enhance your passion and open doors you never thought were imaginable. It may sound nerdy, but it really is fun to learn about things you are interested in and that you are passionate about. When you find what you are passionate about and pursue educational advancement in that area, your life can really become much more fulfilling. In addition to this, the more stuff you know, the easier it is to get through life. Of course you have to get good grades, that's obvious. But focus on truly learning. Gain knowledge about things so that you can enhance your life and expand your horizons. By learning new things you can implement them into your own life and continuously build and create the life you wish to live. Additionally, the more you've learned for yourself the more it will help you share your knowledge and wisdom with others which will then better your own relationships with other people. If you think about it in-depth, by doing this you also better other people's lives which impacts society and the whole world around you.

I've never been the type of person to put a lot of value in having a lot of money and prestigious "things," however I understand the importance of money in our society and the need to have it to survive. I'm not trying to tell you to be greedy and have the most money or to make living in a big house or owning a fancy car your ultimate goals in life. But many people can relate to the fact that having money is necessary, and financial stability or lack thereof plays a pivotal role in the amount of stress and happiness in our lives. I know firsthand the stresses that a lack of money can place on you and your family. Having an education is the first step in eliminating this type of stress.

I believe many Native Americans in general do not pursue higher education for a number of reasons. It's a combination of different things such as lack of opportunity and resources to begin with. I think it also has to do with the history of oppression and unfairness Native

Americans have faced in the past which has unintentionally carried over from generation to generation. In addition, I think many are scared of the unknown as many haven't had someone in their family go to college ahead of them. They may not trust the system or understand what college has to offer. College can be a huge adjustment and is a much different life than life on the reservation. Native Americans are comfortable within their setting, and have a hard time understanding what is beyond what they're used to. Which is definitely not a bad thing because I can relate to that. I honestly didn't want to go far away from home when I was choosing a college, but two of my top choices (Louisville and Columbia) were clear across the country. I didn't want to leave home or my family and I knew it wasn't going to be easy, but I also knew what my goals were. I knew the importance of education and the importance of opportunity and there was no way I would allow myself to miss out on either of those. So I am challenging others to be willing to work hard and take risks for their education and essentially for the benefit of their futures. Educational decisions will help you achieve goals you have for yourself and the life you hope to live — but nothing worthwhile comes from laziness. You have to be disciplined and determined to do well in school and most important you have to remain focused on what you truly want in the end: Would you rather be lazy, take the easy route and hopefully just make it by and live a decent life, OR are you willing to work hard now and eventually live a life you've imagined? The choice is yours but you have to take the initiative.

After being away at college and traveling to countless places, I feel I have a better understanding of different cultures and people. My advice to those considering pursuing a college education is to do it. You have to be willing to change and take a risk by experiencing an unknown. Society and times have changed. You can't live in the past. I understand that as Native Americans we are really hurt by the past, and that inequality and oppression still exist. But there comes a point where either you get past that and move forward or else it just takes over your life. I think the reason a lot of people look up to Shoni and me is because we had the guts to take a risk and step outside of our comfort zone by going away to college. We are living proof that you can leave the reservation and get a college education. It's not easy, but it is very possible for anyone who puts their heart and mind to it. And like I always say, find the positive in it. My mom always used to tell us we could go off and see the world, get our education, and always come back home to the reservation after experiencing what's out there.

I want to give credit to the Native Americans who went off to school while achieving great things ahead of Shoni and me, simply because they helped pave the path and they set an example. Without knowing or meaning to, by setting that example they helped give me and others the confidence to make these types of decisions in order to pursue our education and to take responsibility in the outcome of our future. I hope that as others have done for Shoni and me, that we can be examples for others to go out and pursue their education. I want to see it become a norm that Native Americans go to college. The experience of going to college and getting a degree will change their lives and I have no doubt that Native Americans have the ability to accomplish these things. It will put things into perspective and allow room for a better life. I understand this isn't an easy thing to do – but it is very possible for any Native American (and anyone for that matter) to do with a combination of the right mindset and tools.

TAKING RISKS

If you want something you've never had you must be willing to do something you've never done.

Taking risks is a necessary step in order to gain something you've always wanted but haven't necessarily had the opportunity to pursue. I have three different personal examples I'd like to share that involved taking risks in my life. One of the first risks I remember taking was skipping the 8th grade. My next example is my family's decision to leave the reservation and move to Portland, which was obviously very risky. Another example is my decision to attend college all the way across the country. Each of these examples had the possibility to go in the wrong direction but through integrity, hard work, and determination they all paid off.

Each of these held different levels of riskiness, and they all demonstrate times in my life I either chose to get out of my comfort zone or life sort of forced me to. I had no other options other than taking the risk and growing, or allowing myself to remain where I was and who I was and settling for less than what I knew was my absolute best.

Luckily for me, I found a way to take the risks and grow as an individual. When I decided to skip the 8th grade I had no idea it would go as smoothly as it did. I also know that if I didn't take that risk my life would've turned out very differently. I would've only played two years of high school sports with my sister, and I quite possibly would've chosen a different college. I also doubt I would've had the exact opportunities I've been blessed with over the last few years. My family's decision to leave the reservation was the hardest risk I've ever been a part of. Being Native American and leaving the reservation is a big step and an even bigger change to adjust to, but even more so, being a Native American and being extremely close to your family and then going off to college 2,000 miles away from home is a whole other risk in itself. All three of these times I really had no idea what to expect and going into it all I had no idea what was going to happen with my life. But I know that if I hadn't had the courage to take these risks my life would probably be very different from what it is today.

What I want people to learn from my example is that taking risks to better your life is a must. You can't allow doubt, uncertainty, or fear to dictate the decisions you make. You have to focus on all of the good that could possibly come from your risk-taking. Many times people naturally become overwhelmed by what could go wrong but letting that stop you would be the easy thing to do. It's easy to stress and constantly worry about what bad things might happen if you decide to make this kind of life-changing choice, but I can say from personal experience there will always be something good that comes from taking a risk. Obviously I have taken more risks in my life than the three I have mentioned, but my whole point here is that not every risk I've taken has gone perfectly or how I hoped it would. For example, I originally thought that my risk to go off to college and play basketball with my sister was going to be the best experience of my life. Although it eventually became that, it wasn't always that way. My freshman year was a terrible experience and I honestly was not happy. But even though it wasn't going how I hoped it would I learned a lot from it. I made myself realize that not everything is going to go how you planned and that you have to learn to adjust to it all. My point again is that there is always something good that comes from taking risks: either it turns out to be something that becomes extremely beneficial and life changing for you, or you simply learn from it and appreciate the experience it gave you. Even if it doesn't go as planned, once you've had that experience you have gotten yourself one step closer to figuring out what it takes to get to where you want to be. Taking risks can be scary -- trust me, I know -- but we can't allow our fear to consume us. Learn to get outside your comfort zone and grow. And take a risk to better your life because you deserve it. Things that challenge us will only help us grow as individuals and that's really what life is about: it's about growing and slowly becoming the person you were meant to be and eventually living the life you were meant to live.

The last thing I want to talk about is getting outside of your comfort zone. In some cases this is the same thing as taking a risk but in another sense it is different. Getting outside your comfort zone will prepare you and help you deal with the unexpected things in life. And being able to do it shows strength and courage. If you aren't willing to do this you may just miss out on opportunities that could be very helpful and sometimes life changing. Being an introvert and a shy person, I know what it's like to want to be comfortable and how hard it can be to put yourself in unfamiliar situations, but once you do it you really do begin to see a good change. When my family and I first started traveling to different reservations and communities to share our story with Native Americans and to speak about different things, I maybe spoke for about 30 seconds or a minute. I used to be terrified of public speaking and I would avoid it at all costs, but over time because I've made myself do it more and more, I've become more comfortable with it. And the way I look at it is that if I hadn't made myself speak longer and more often, in a sense that would be selfish of me and I would not be in the position I am today. I probably wouldn't be recognized as one of the most influential or inspiring Native Americans across the country. I'm not by any means trying to credit myself or brag. All I'm trying to do is paint a picture for others to understand that trying new things will change your situation for the better. It will help you grow as an individual and it will give you the chance to have opportunities that you wouldn't even have imagined. Risk taking isn't easy; it's actually quite scary. But if it is a step toward bettering your life then do it. If you take risks you give yourself the chance to gain something great. If it doesn't work out at least you tried and at least you learned from it. But if it does, your whole life will completely change and you will be so happy and thankful that you were strong enough and brave enough to do it.

BALANCE

Extremes are easy. Strive for balance.

In my opinion one of the most important, yet one of the hardest, things to maintain in life is balance. Balance is so essential to life that I can't stress it enough. We can't be too focused on one thing too much or it will begin to throw off the balance of our lives. I've witnessed other people do this, and I've also experienced it personally. I used to focus on things that weren't necessarily going to make my life what I wanted it to be. At one point in my life I used to spend much of my time worried about one particular relationship, and that took up a lot of my focus. I also used to focus on how unfairly we were treated as a Native American family in a predominantly white social setting. However, as I grew up, I slowly began to realize that life is about variety, versatility and balance. You can't get too caught up in anything. Remember your goals and your dreams, and stay focused on them. But also realize that there is still a need for healthy fun, leisure, and relaxation.

That's one thing I've learned over the last few years on my own, but I also remember my parents used to practice and preach this as well. When it's time to work and get things done that should be your only focus. But there has to be time and room for a break. You have to treat yourself every once in a while. You have to hang out with friends and have fun. There is nothing wrong with that so long as it's healthy fun. I know a lot of people think drinking, drugs, and partying are either fun or an escape from their real life, but I promise they're not positive things. I'm not a saint - I've had my fair share of "fun" - but I eventually realized there are healthy ways to enjoy myself. Drinking and drugs only hurt you personally and negatively affect those around you. Another way to think about it is that they are just additional obstacles keeping you from reaching your goals. If you can't stay away from those temptations for your sake, please do it for your family and friends. Think about your family. Think about your siblings, your grandparents, your parents and all those you care about. You may have seen and witnessed the problems associated with drugs and alcohol firsthand at some point in your life. And of course all races have dealt with these types of issues, but Native Americans have been stereotyped for using drugs and alcohol for decades because the problem undoubtedly exists. Furthermore, it has limited our chances to succeed and be happy. I know there are many different points of view when it comes to the justification of this issue, but our people have suffered long enough from using and abusing substances. Life has so many positive things to offer that we shouldn't have to turn to drugs and alcohol. Be healthy and do healthy things.

It's so easy to give into temptation, and oftentimes that can lead directly to steering you away from the life of your dreams. It's easy to do what's fun. It's easy to be lazy. It's easy to get bad grades. It's easy to give into peer pressure. It's easy to do all these things. But I want to see change. I want to see Native Americans have the strength to eliminate these things from their lives and begin to thrive and go after their goals and dreams. If you take a step back it's actually quite easy. The process of getting what you want out of life is simple. We can't allow the struggles and stresses of everyday life to take over our minds and emotions. I've learned if you can control your thoughts everything else will fall into place. It sounds cliché but it's true. Positive thoughts will turn into positive behavior, and positive behavior will lead to positive outcomes. But, as always, it takes focus, desire, determination, and resilience. As minorities, Native Americans may have to work one hundred times harder than their peers to achieve their goals, but don't let that discourage you. If we truly want to see change for our people, we have to begin to make these changes and set higher standards. We have to fight for what we want. And more than anything, we have to believe it's possible. It's all a process and I know we can do it. It has to be one small change at a time, one day at a time, and one person at a time. Then we will get there. Like I said earlier, healthy balance is essential.

Therefore, stay happy, stay healthy, and keep your life balanced.

PART 2: MY LESSONS

HEALTH

Love yourself enough to live a healthy lifestyle.

Although there are different aspects to health (mind, body, spirit) each one is equally important. Health involves all aspects of the human body, mind, and many other things that concern the wellbeing of someone. When it comes down to it, these types of things are in your control. Other people who love and care about you and your health can turn blue in the face trying to tell you what is right and what is wrong, but deep down inside you know what's good for you and what's bad for you. Just like you know what is healthy for you and what isn't. Each of us needs to understand that there is absolutely no such thing as perfection, and there isn't anybody who does absolutely everything right or perfectly all of the time. We're humans and we are naturally drawn to flaw and temptation. But so long as we learn from our mistakes and our experiences then everything will be okay.

As I was saying, health involves multiple factors and that is important to know and understand. You have to fuel each one of these things the right way in order to gain and maintain good health. Your food choices have an impact on your health, as well as your exercise routine. Your consciousness and awareness of your own thoughts and feelings also play a significant role in your overall health. When it comes to your diet and your weight, the biggest thing is that you have to understand your body and you have to understand that you are different than any other person. There is no reason to compare your body type or your eating habits to that of others. Obviously there are the simple and basic things when it comes to food and nutrition, such as everyone should drink plenty of water, eat fruits and vegetables, etc. There are helpful tools such as the food pyramid to help guide us in the right direction, and also to help us understand the things our bodies need in order to be healthy and maintain this health. It's not always about the quantity of food, but the quality of what you are putting inside your body. And it's not necessarily about eating less, but more so about eating what's right for you. Also, working out can be a challenge - especially when you are first starting out or if you have a busy schedule. I've read many times that the number one reason why people don't work out is because of a perceived lack of time which is why time management is so important. There are only twenty-four hours in a day and only seven days in a week, but ultimately we make time for the things we truly care about. And you should care enough about yourself to make time to take care of your body.

It is important that you find a way to stay active, because your physical fitness is very important to your overall health. Not everyone is the same when it comes to their motivation levels or enjoyment of exercise and there are some athletes and fitness junkies who love working out and put in countless hours of exercise. However, this difference cannot be the reason you choose to avoid exercising. It's not about comparing yourself to the fanatics; it's simply about improving and increasing your health. If you're someone who may not enjoy working out or has a busy schedule, my advice is to find an activity you do enjoy and try to plan out your days and weeks in advance. I'm confident everyone can find twenty minutes just a few times a week if you make it a priority. Exercise can take many fun forms, including riding a bike, playing basketball, etc. Remember it doesn't have to be anything in particular, just get out there and be active because it's important for your health.

When it comes to appropriate exercising and good eating habits, discipline plays an important role. Therefore you must find the strength in yourself to be self-disciplined and be in control of yourself, your eating habits, and your exercising routine. And most important be stronger than all of the excuses that may come up. Anybody can find an excuse as to why they don't eat well or why they don't exercise adequately, but at some point we need to realize that these excuses are the only thing holding us back from becoming a healthier individual. Another thing to think about is the fact that what we are fueling our bodies with right now and what our exercising habits are right now will affect us and our lives down the road. Therefore think about it like this: you can be undisciplined now and eat all the junk food you want, drink all the soda you want, and never exercise, but eventually these things will catch up to you, and nobody wants to deal with an unhealthy body or the effects of unhealthy habits when they get older. I feel like because of the increase and advancement of medicine and technology, people tend to rely more than they should on medication, plastic surgery, or other cures. We often forget that most of the time we can prevent sickness and prevent our bodies from becoming something we don't appreciate simply by making healthier choices and controlling what we can control. Again, I understand that everybody is different. Genetics play a part in our body types and things like our immune system, but at the end of the day every individual needs to be focused on themselves. We need to stay focused on being the healthiest we can be personally and not waste time comparing ourselves to someone or something we aren't.

Next, I want to talk again about the effect of drugs and alcohol. To me it just doesn't make sense why humans want to do these types of things to themselves when in reality all it really does is deteriorate our bodies and brains. As I've said before it's easy to be pressured or tempted to take part in these things and for some people it's a habit or a hobby. Of course everyone is going to do what they please but what I'm saying is either don't do it at all or be disciplined enough to do it in moderation and don't allow it to consume you, your health, and your life. There's a time, a place, and an age for these types of things, but if it were up to me I would just tell people to stay away from it regardless of the reason they do it or why they are involved in it. I know some people do it because it helps them deal with stress or because they are depressed or because they are peer pressured into it or simply because they think it's cool, but here's how I see it: either your choices are reflecting the kind of life you want to live and helping you get there or they are hurting you and only taking you further from the life you hope to have or the life you should be living.

I know it may sound like I'm preaching but I'm just so tired of seeing people allow these habits to take over their lives. You're stronger than that. And you have the power to stay away from this negativity. For those who may already be caught up in these things, you have the power to walk away from them. And you deserve better than that. You deserve to live a happy and healthy life and everyone else in the world can tell you that but it will never truly begin to happen until you yourself believe it and begin to make changes toward becoming a better, stronger individual. And another thing to take into consideration is the fact that what you do doesn't affect just you. It impacts everyone around you. Your family, your friends, your community, and everybody else. Think about that. Think about how your actions could be influencing the ones you love and care about, and on top of doing it for yourself use this as motivation to work toward becoming the best possible you that you can be. Don't take the easy route. Don't be weak. Challenge yourself to grow and become stronger. Do it for those you love and care about most and most important do it for yourself because you deserve it and you deserve to live a life full of health and happiness.

The last piece I would like to talk about in this section is the mind and how significant it is. Most people these days are more than aware of the physical side of health, but what we think, meaning the psychological side of things, is just as important (if not more so) to our overall wellbeing. What we think, especially about ourselves, has a huge impact on our health. Just like food and drinks, our emotions and our thoughts are also fuel into our overall health, and those can either be good or bad depending on what we allow to take place inside our heads. Honestly, this is the hardest part when it comes to being healthy. It's very difficult to convince yourself to think a certain way and feel a certain way and act a certain way. But it's all in our mind. It takes a lot of discipline and really it just takes a lot of self-love. If we truly love and care about ourselves as much as we preach that we should, then things would be simple. All we would have to do is make the right choice and not look back on it, then eventually things will fall into place.

So I am challenging each of you to start training yourself and making yourself think a certain way. Once you do this your feelings and actions will all follow suit. Again, I've seen countless numbers of people allowing their thoughts and emotions to control their lives and their situations, and I've dealt with similar struggles myself. But at some point we have to find the strength in us and decide that trying to do what is right and live a happier and healthier life is much more meaningful and important than whatever negativity may be affecting us. Whether it's school, work, stress, sports, drugs, alcohol, relationships, etc., you have to decide that none of that negativity even comes close to the significance of trying to make yourself a better, healthier, happier person living a life you've wanted or imagined for yourself. This might be a touchy subject but I know that a lot of people suffer from overwhelming stress, and things like loneliness, depression, and thoughts of suicide begin to creep in. I promise you whatever it may be that is causing you to feel this way will get better, but it won't do that if you are feeling sorry for yourself and allowing yourself to stay stuck there. I know that between the everyday struggles and the ups and downs of life as well as the rare crazy and traumatic experiences some people are faced with that life isn't easy. It's actually quite hard at times. But I promise you "for every dark night there is a brighter day." There is always a way to try and better your life and your situation. Find that small piece of positivity, hold onto it tight and then build off it. Eventually it will become bigger and bigger and you will find yourself in a much better place both mentally and physically.

In conclusion I just want to say that you have to love yourself. And you have to have enough love for yourself to set your physical and mental health as significant priorities in your life because at the end of the day your health is the most prized possession any of us have. All the money, cars, clothes, and other superficial things in our lives can't and never will amount to the richness and importance of our health. Therefore, if you take anything from this theme just remember to love yourself and take responsibility for your overall health because it will all impact the outcome of your life. After all, you deserve to live the healthiest, happiest, and best life possible. The last thing I want to say is to remember whatever you choose to do and every choice you make is either getting you further from where you want to be or helping you get closer to it.

PART 2: MY LESSONS

INTEGRITY

Real integrity is doing the right thing,
knowing that nobody's going to know whether you did it or not.
– Oprah Winfrey

I feel like many people lose track of one of the most important qualities anyone can have. Integrity is arguably the most valuable characteristic someone can possess, or at least it is in my opinion. Because without it nothing else really matters: all the money, all the success, happiness, and everything else is nothing without integrity. Nowadays for the majority of people it seems like it's all about being successful and doing what you have to do in order to get to the top or to make money. But in my opinion and generally speaking our society lacks integrity. Even though it's a very simple concept people still can't seem to make it a top priority when really it should be our most valued moral. Most people talk a good game and this will only get you so far if your actions don't go hand in hand with whatever it is you're saying. Also, many people do good things in front of others but then behind closed doors they aren't the same type of person. One of my favorite sayings is that what you do in front of others means nothing if you are living a different life behind closed doors.

There are so many things I could say about integrity, but I want to keep this theme short because to me it's very simple: either do what is good or you do what is wrong. And as I've said before, deep down inside every single one of us knows what is right and what is wrong, therefore don't try to make it more complicated than it needs to be. Too many people lack the values we need. Everyone talks about change and talks about wanting to see the world fair and equal but it starts with individuals. If you can't make yourself do what is right all the time, what makes you think the systems and institutions within society are going to do that? Life isn't fair and people don't always do what is right. But having integrity will begin to make that change. Do what is right and do it even if you don't want to, because selfishness and personal gain will only get you so far. Of course we need to look out for ourselves and protect ourselves but if we know in our hearts the difference between good and bad and right or wrong, then regardless of societal issues you need to do what is right and not what is easy.

This is the case when it comes to everything and anything in your life. When it comes to your honesty and trust in others and your relationships with them -- whether it's job or work related, whether it has to do with the law or something as small as littering. I could go into very specific detail about all of these things but at the end of the day it comes down to you and the choices you make; how you choose to behave and the things you choose to do. I'm not saying everything the society promotes is right. I know there are many things that aren't fair or okay that are still taking place today in all aspects of life (governmental, economic, social, etc.) I'm aware that our society is slightly naïve and ignorant at times but adding fuel to the fire won't get you to where you want to be. Fighting fire with fire will only burn you in the long run. Two wrongs don't make a right, and I am challenging anyone who reads this book to do what is right regardless of the situation or outcome. I'm not saying allow others to run all over you or allow them to control your life. In my opinion the integrity of your character has absolutely nothing to do with anyone but yourself, and there is a difference between character and reputation. Your concern should be your character. Worry about the purity of yourself and your actions because that is what you have to live with. Your reputation is only what others think of you and you can only control that by the actions you take.

PART 3: MY PEOPLE

_____

In the following pages of Part III,

I want to briefly discuss Native Americans

in a variety of ways in order to portray them

more accurately than they have been in the past.

I truly want to help others understand

the culture of a minority group

that has been unfairly stereotyped for generations.

Most important I want everyone,

including Native Americans themselves,

to see the beauty and potential they possess.

PART 3: MY PEOPLE

UNDERSTANDING NATIVE AMERICANS

I believe Native Americans are a very misunderstood people. I wanted to write this part of the book to help show others what Native American people and the culture are about. It is very important to me that people realize the inaccuracies and incorrect stereotypes and assumptions that are still prevalent today regarding Native Americans. There is so much more to the history and present state of Native people across the country than most people realize, and I wanted to help them better understand by giving insight from my perspective.

Native Americans are beautiful, smart, talented, and deserving people. They have huge hearts, and believe that respect for themselves and for others is extremely important. They believe in what's truly and purely right. They believe in integrity and always doing the right thing. They also believe in the idea that what you give is what you will get. The concept of karma does exist and what you put out into the world is what you will get back.

Native Americans believe in camaraderie and unity. Society has somehow found a way to create divisions among different groups of people in all aspects you can think of: race, politics, religion, economics, and everything else. Native Americans don't believe in these divisions among humans. Rather, they believe in working together to create a life of equality and goodness, which will benefit all individuals and not just one particular group of people.

The balance between mind, body, and soul is important to Native Americans as well. They believe each of these works together and need to be in harmony with one another in order to live a healthy and happy life. They believe that you have to take care of and respect yourself in all manners, because what you think, feel, and say on the inside will manifest on the outside.

Respect is extremely important for Native Americans in all aspects but, especially towards nature. Nature is very sacred and significant because it is essential to survival. Celebrating the land has been a tradition in Native American lives since the beginning of time. Natives believe that the earth is pure and necessary. They believe that living off of Mother Earth is crucial, and therefore they should show her the utmost respect. Natives have sincere reverence for everything on this earth because it is believed that it all serves a purpose. Throughout history, animals such as buffalo, deer, elk, and fish were hunted and fished, which was a way for food and survival. Roots, berries, and plants are also celebrated as they provided sources of food for Native Americans. Even things that seem simple and pointless to many non-Natives are believed to serve a purpose. For example, rocks and fire may seem insignificant, but they were important in early life for Native Americans, and demanded respect and value from them.

Native Americans highly value their faith in God, also known as the creator. They also care dearly for their families, especially the elders and future generations. Praying and giving thanks for all they have and Mother Nature is important. Also, Native Americans believe everyone was put on this earth for a reason that is greater than themselves.

I feel like people think it's easy to pressure, control, or dictate and take advantage of Native Americans. It is not because we aren't strong and smart. It's simply because of our values. It's in our nature to be good people and have good hearts. Many people value the logic and rationality of the brain, which is definitely important, but Native Americans have always been about using their gut feelings and following their hearts. There is a time and place to think with your brain and be logical; that's undeniable. However, it may be because the heart can perceive bad or evil. It's typical to think logically and allow reasoning to make you greedy and selfish. Just look at the values of our society today. Of course this isn't inclusive of all people in the world, but our current society has a value system, which encourages these types of things. That is exactly why oppression, economic gaps, educational gaps, and racial gaps exist. Capitalism and consumerism have become the norms within society. Many people look at Native Americans and question whether they truly desire to become successful. However, it's not that we don't want to have large amounts of money, big houses, and nice cars. It's just a matter of differing values and traditions. Native Americans have always valued the things many people seem to now take for granted. For example, as mentioned previously, Natives value things such as nature, thinking with your heart, always respecting themselves and others, and doing what is truly best for the greater good. I actually believe the rest of the world could learn a lot from Native American values.

In addition, there are plenty of other reasons why Native Americans are not as successful as they should be: the lack of opportunity; the lack of role models; the lack of courage. Native Americans tend to get the short end of the stick. Some people may argue that they get money from the government or they get other special benefits - but that's unfair. Native Americans were living a pure and simple life in this country before anything else happened here. Their land was taken from them. They were repeatedly mistreated. Millions of Native Americans were murdered, and the rest were forced into living on reservations and living under rules and legislation that were forced upon them by the government of European settlers. It's not like all of this just happened overnight. It's not like Native Americans just decided they didn't want to be successful. There are various and undeniable factors that play into these issues. Native Americans rarely get the opportunity to be exposed to things that will give them the chance to live a successful life (such as the ability to get a higher education and a good job). A lot of reservations are in extremely rural places which makes it even harder to accomplish these things.

For the most part, Native Americans are only exposed to certain things and for quite some time they just simply haven't known anything more than that. Every other race has numerous role models and leaders who are well known for their youth to look up to and attempt to emulate. Native Americans lack these role models. I'm not saying there haven't been any successful or influential Native Americans because there have been. People like Jim Thorpe and Billy Mills, tribal leaders, actors, writers, designers, etc. are examples of some individuals who have made their mark and have been role models for other Native Americans. My point is that there are not enough role models, and that directly stems from broader problems within Native American communities. There aren't enough Native Americans who are graduating from high school, going to college, and getting jobs. It's a mixture of various factors that have influenced this cycle of life, but people can't pretend that it's all a coincidence or that it is simply a choice by Native Americans for things to be this way. Native Americans also face a disproportionate number of issues such as poverty, depression, alcohol, drugs, oppression, discrimination, lack of education, and lack of opportunity. I've witnessed these issues firsthand both during my years on the reservation in Oregon and also on the numerous trips I've taken to other Native American tribes and communities.

It is also important that non-Natives learn to understand the diversity among Native people. There are numerous differences and subcultures within the Native American culture. Currently, there are more than

500 Native American tribes recognized by the government. Each of these tribes is unique in their own way. They have different languages, traditions, teachings, locations, populations, and distributions of land and money. Going back in time a bit, there were also different methods of survival that contributed to each tribe's ways of life and culture. For example, the location, climate, weather, environment, and the resources are all key factors that play into the way in which Natives used to live. The Native Americans who lived in the northwest obviously lived a different lifestyle and had different methods of survival (such as how they fed themselves, clothed themselves, what type of homes they lived in/built, etc.) than those who lived in the southern or eastern hemispheres of the country.

Oftentimes, those who don't know very much about Native Americans base their understandings off of inaccurate assumptions and stereotypes. For example, some have asked, "Do you still live in tipis?" The answer is no. At one point in time this was the case, but as society developed, Native Americans had to evolve in some aspects just like everyone else. These types of misunderstandings don't help Native Americans when it comes to the struggle of receiving opportunities or achieving success. This is why I think it's so important for Native Americans to make changes. Natives need to change the cycle they are going through so that we can get educations and start gaining power, status, and prestige. It's not about having control or superiority but more so when these things start to happen, we can begin to teach others accurately and influence them in a positive manner.

While being away from reservation life or in the so-called "real world," I often feel that people I meet look to me to know or educate them about every detail of Native Americans. I definitely can say that I don't know everything that there is to know and understand, because I don't. The knowledge I am sharing in this book is simply based off my own experiences. I'm still learning to this very day. Even though there is a pretty firm foundation of similarities among Native Americans, when I have had the privilege and opportunity to go visit and speak at different tribes, reservations, and communities around the country I always learned new things, saw new places, gained new experiences, and met new people. For example, some tribes do ceremonies such as the sun dance, which is the celebration of the transition from childhood into adulthood. Other tribes have different ceremonies, or no ceremonies at all. This is just a vague example of how not all Native American tribes are the same when it comes to specific traditions.

In my opinion after visiting countless tribes, there are still lots of similarities amongst Native Americans and amongst each of the different tribes. Native Americans seem to all have strong hearts, regardless of region. They were all affected by the past and history of their people. They all believe in respect and honor. They all believe in a greater or higher power. They believe in respect of nature and everything this world has to offer. Even if humans are susceptible to wrongdoing and committing sin, Native Americans believe in integrity and the greater good. You're not supposed to contribute to the negative energy of the world. Rather you are to focus on making it a better place and living out the purpose of your life.

Of course there is no single way to explain why Native Americans are the way they are or how they got that way. Like I said, it's a mixture of many different factors. And again, there are many differences among Native Americans, which is important for people to understand. The most important thing, however, is that people realize the inaccuracy of assumptions and stereotypes often attributed to Natives. These are not reliable, and there is much more to the history and present state of Native Americans across the country than many people understand.

As I've mentioned before I am not an expert and I don't claim to know everything. Rather I wanted to include this part of the book to help others to gain a better understanding of Native American history and culture in hopes that my insight will lead to more opportunities for others to live happily, healthfully, and successfully.

CONCLUSION:

_____

DREAMCATCHER

The symbolism of the Dreamcatcher is perfect for the concept and purpose of my book. Dreamcatchers can be considered a Native American tradition that date back generations. It is believed that dreamcatchers filter out all of the bad dreams while we are sleeping, and only allow positive dreams and good thoughts to enter our minds. Dreamcatchers are also a symbol of unity and strength.

I started out this book by sharing my story and some of my personal experiences over the years. I did this in order to help paint a picture for others to realize and understand that factors such as where you come from and the things that happen to you do not necessarily determine where you can go with your life and what you can accomplish. I didn't share things about my life to show off what I've accomplished or to brag about my family or myself. Rather, I shared these things because I want to display myself as an example for others to see that their dreams are possible to reach. By sharing my story and experiences, I wanted to simply provide a sense of hope, positivity, and inspiration for others. I want them to put aside all forms of negativity and realize their true strength so that they can begin to take control of their lives and make a difference for themselves, those they love, and for the greater good.

I chose to include a part that portrayed my insight on various matters of life. And to be very honest I questioned whether or not all of these things were common sense. But the more I thought about it, the more it made sense to share with the world the lessons I learned through my own experiences because I wanted people to see that I've dealt with similar situations as the ones they are going through. This part of the book included lessons my parents taught me while I was growing up, combined with things that I learned on my own simply through the unique life experiences that I was exposed to. I chose to include this section because I feel as though many people, myself included, allow life to get the best of them at times. And to me this is why so many people never really live the life they've imagined for themselves. I wrote this part of the book in hopes of providing others with insight and knowledge that will help them take a step back from the stresses of life and realize how simple it can be. I want others to understand that life is only as complex as we make it. And most importantly, I want others to understand that everything we need to make it in life is within ourselves. Life is full of ups and downs, goods and bads, and all other forms of contradictions. My hope is that others will implement these insights into their own lives so that they can give themselves the opportunity to catch their dreams. Life is going to happen, nature is going to run its course, and the time is going to pass, but we need to realize that we only get one life to live. I don't want anyone to settle for anything less than what they deserve. And that begins when we realize that it's all as simple as we choose to make it.

I was also compelled to include a section to help others to get a feel for Native Americans and what we stand for, our culture, and our unique ways of life. It's been my experience that many non-Natives don't know very much about Native Americans, and the information they do know is usually inaccurate. By including this information, I want others to dispose of previous assumptions and to understand the true essence of Native Americans. I hope to teach others and inspire others to understand that there is much more to Native Americans than what is understood, and also to realize Native Americans are still in an oppressed state that is often ignored. I also hope to inspire other Native Americans to go out and share the beauty of our heritage with the rest of the world.

Most important to me, the overall purpose of my book is to inspire hope. And I am challenging each and every one of you to strive for greatness. I'm challenging you to put aside everything that is holding you back, and to do whatever it takes to live a happy, healthy, and successful life. Change won't happen overnight, I think we all know that, but with one step at a time we really can begin to not only better our own lives, but also we can begin to create a society of integrity and equality. I know there have been others before myself who have encouraged and fought for what is right and that is my only intention. Divisions mean nothing to me. This is about unity. This is about acceptance. And this is about equality.

Ever since I was a young girl, I've had the dream to be in a position to change the world. By writing this book, I hope to be a difference maker. I'm aware that there has yet to be exclusive goodness and unity among all people in our society, but there is absolutely no reason we can't strive for that. And that is the ultimate dream I wish to achieve: unity and positivity for all. Through my experiences and lessons I've learned, I've been able to catch many of my dreams. Just like the Dreamcatcher, I hope this book can be a symbol of unity and strength, and also play a part in helping you filter out the negatives in your life while letting the positives shine through.

CENTER FOR NATIVE AMERICAN YOUTH
AT THE ASPEN INSTITUTE

www.CNAY.org
GenI@cnay.org
Twitter: Center4Native

Generation Indigenous

President Obama announced the establishment of the Generation Indigenous (Gen-I) initiative on December 3, 2014. Gen-I is focused on removing the barriers that stand between Native youth and their opportunity to succeed. Learn more about Gen-I at **www.cnay.org/Gen-I_Overview.html**.

Take the Gen-I Challenge
cnay.org/Challenge.html

Sign up as a Youth Ambassador

Facebook.com/GenIndigenous
Twitter: @Gen_Indigenous

Native Youth Network

As a part of Gen-I, the Center for Native American Youth created the Native Youth Network. The Network provides a framework to map programs serving Native youth & connect young people with resources. The goals of the Network are to:

- Build and maintain a platform to elevate Native youth voices.
- Increase Native youth access to scholarships, trainings, mentors, and support.
- Connect Native youth to each other in a leadership network.

Youth Ambassadors

Youth Ambassadors act as liaisons to share resources and opportunities with peers and communities. Ambassadors are a part of a growing Gen-I Network of community leaders and serve as direct connections to communities and perspectives on Native youth priorities. Reach out, take the challenge, and join the Ambassadors!